Herb Mixtures
& Spicy Blends

Introduction by Maggie Oster

Edited by Deborah L. Balmuth

A Storey Publishing Book

 Storey Communications, Inc.
Pownal, Vermont 05261

*The mission of Storey Communications is to serve our customers
by publishing practical information that encourages
personal independence in harmony with the environment.*

Cover & text design by Cynthia N. McFarland
Cover photograph by A. Blake Gardner
Text production by Cynthia N. McFarland and Susan Bernier
Indexed by Northwind Editorial Services

Printed in the United States by R.R. Donnelley

10 9 8 7 6 5 4 3 2 1

Library of Congress Cataloging-in-Publication Data

Herb mixtures & spicy blends / introduction by Maggie Oster: edited by
  Deborah Balmuth
        p.   cm.
      "A Storey Publishing Book"
      Includes bibliographical references and index.
        ISBN 0-88266-919-2 (hc: alk. paper). — ISBN 0-88266-918-4
(pbk.: alk paper)
      1. Cookery (Herbs) 2. Herbs. 3. Spices. I. Balmuth, Deborah L.,
1955-   .
TX819.H4H4542   1996
641.6'57— dc20   95-52092
                                                                CIP

Contents

Introduction

Maggie Oster

t the end of the day when I'm tired and dragging in the kitchen, I like to either steam or lightly sauté vegetables. Ready-made herb and spice mixtures introduce ease and simplicity into this kind of cooking. Just add a little water, sprinkle on some herb blend, and — presto! — you have a dinner that tastes good and is different from the usual, without a lot of advance planning. Moreover, by using more herbs to flavor food, you use less salt and oil in your cooking — eliminating calories and boosting your health.

Herb blends are great for turning ordinary dishes into something special. Having your own favorite homemade blends on hand opens up all kinds of flavor possibilities. Plain old steamed vegetables may be a bit boring, but with a selection of herb blends on hand, you have the choice of all kinds of flavors — depending on the blend and your mood — and instead of pulling out eighteen different spice jars to get your combination, you just need one! Simple appetizers like cheese balls and dips, hamburgers, and pastas with sautéed vegetables take on more exciting, unexpected flavors with a sprinkle of your own homemade herb or spice blend.

This collection of recipes from herb growers and buyers across North America reveals the great versatility of herb and spice blends.

There are great multipurpose savory blends to sprinkle on chicken before you stick it in the oven. There are also recipes for more unexpected blends — for desserts, quick breads, muffins and scones, biscuits, and all those kinds of things. You can even add one of the dessert blends to cobblers and pies. Cobblers are really fast desserts to prepare, and they can be served quite elegantly with some good ice cream in a stemmed glass.

Reading through these recipes, I'm inspired by the wide range of blends and surprised by all the recipe possibilities you have with just a few blends. I've gotten some great ideas just as I browse through them. Sometimes a recipe suggests a couple of different herbs that I wouldn't have thought about using, sparking me to try some new combinations. It's easy for any of us to get into a rut with our cooking; herb blends are a great way to break old habits.

What I love about this book is that it includes everything from soup to nuts — great suggestions for everything from brightening up salads to making dynamite-hot chili, scrumptious pumpkin pie, and your own special herb tea. I hope you have fun with it!

Using Herb Mixtures & Spicy Blends

Making the most of the wide array of herb and spice blends takes a bit of practice — "getting into the herbal habit" is the best way I can think of to summarize it. If you're grilling a hamburger, chicken breast, or lamb chop, add some herbs, either by putting them in a marinade or sprinkling them on top. That's the beginning of the herbal habit. But what's really fun is to think of more inventive ways to incorporate herb and spice blends into your everyday eating.

For instance, oven roasting is a fun technique. It's so simple, and it's a wonderful, fairly quick, and easy way to have dinner. You can oven roast anything from marinated tofu to potatoes, sweet potatoes, turnips, onions, zucchini, and mushrooms. Just add a little bit of olive oil, your choice of herb mixture, and coat all the pieces evenly. Put it in the oven at 350°F, wait half an hour, and you've got dinner. The flavor is so much more than that of steamed vegetables, and if you use just 1 to 2 tablespoons of oil, the increased calories are really only marginal.

Low-Fat Options

Making your own herbed cheese is a great way to use herb blends — except that nobody eats cheese any more. A good low-calorie alternative is yogurt cheese. This is also great for people with lactose intolerance.

The simplest way to make yogurt cheese, if you don't have the official cheesemaker sieve, is to line a strainer with cheesecloth, pour in the plain yogurt, and let it drain for a couple of hours or overnight. The result is like cream cheese, and it's good! Yogurt works well on herb toast or briochette and can be very flavorful when mixed with any of the multipurpose or some of the special herb blends. Also consider using nonfat ricotta, sour cream, or mayonnaise products.

A baked potato isn't much with just a sprinkling of dried herbs, but if you first blend the herbs with nonfat sour cream, and then put that on your potato, you've got something really good.

The nonfat products aren't always good for cooking and the flavor isn't as rich as the full-fat version, but with the addition of an herb mixture, you can lower the fat without losing the flavor.

Low-fat salad dressings are easy to make with herb mixtures. I like to use 2 parts oil to 1 part vinegar, or even 1 part to 1 part.

When to add the herbs depends on the type of recipe. For spread, dips, and dressings, it's better if the flavors have time to blend and meld. Meat seasonings are usually added before cooking, while the no-salt mixtures are usually sprinkled on near the end of cooking or used at the table in place of salt.

Purchasing Herbs

You can find a growing selection of dried herbs in your supermarket spice rack, but the prices tend to be prohibitive, particularly for making blends in bulk to give as gifts. There are two primary

places for purchasing dried herbs inexpensively in bulk: herb farms or shops and health food stores. Often, gourmet or specialty food shops and cooking stores also sell dried herbs inexpensively in small-bulk quantities.

There are mail-order suppliers of dried herbs, including some of the herb shops profiled in this book. So if you don't have a local supplier, you may want to buy from one of the mail-order suppliers listed on page 139.

When buying in bulk, it's tempting to get a sackful. However, don't purchase too much since one of the keys to quality blends is not storing them too long. Six months is the ideal shelf life for dried herbs, although one year is the maximum before they really start to lose flavor. So be cautious about how much you buy, unless you're making presents and can use the large quantity quickly.

One more tip: If you have a choice of buying dried herbs in whole leaf form, I recommend it. This allows you to grind them yourself to the desired consistency. However, buying herbs already ground is also quite acceptable. Then the blending process just involves making sure all the ingredients are mixed well.

Drying Your Own Fresh Herbs

If you ask me, everybody should grow their own herbs! It's easy and simple. You can buy most herb plants at a nursery and plant them in a garden or in containers. If desired, you could also buy freshly harvested herbs at the grocery store and dry them yourself, although this can get expensive. See the "Related Books" list on page 146 for basic information on growing herbs.

Drying is probably the most popular way of preserving herbs, and it's easy, as well. The best possible scenario is to pick herbs just as they're coming into bloom. But I find life complicated enough without having to worry about picking my herbs on time, so I harvest them whenever I can. A good test is to take a nibble and see if the herb's flavor is good; if so, go ahead and harvest. It's best to pick herbs early in the morning after the dew has dried. If you have mulched beds, the herbs probably don't need to be washed. If they do need washing, I recommend picking while the herbs are still damp with dew, washing, shaking off as much water as possible, and then spreading them out to dry on towels.

Once the herbs are dry, strip off the leaves as gently as possible. By pulling off the leaves first, you don't have to mess with the stems at all. It's important to be gentle because the more times the leaves are bruised at any stage of the process, the more oils are lost. There are several ways to harvest gently. One method is to hang up the stems in little bunches and put them in a cool, dark place to dry before removing leaves. Generally, I like to take the fresh leaves off the stems very carefully, spread them out on non-stick cookie sheets in as thin a layer as possible (ideally just one layer thick), and put them in an oven set at the lowest possible temperature. I use cookie sheets because that's what I have, but screens work particularly well.

Depending on the size of the leaf and the moisture content, fresh herbs will take anywhere from a couple of hours to overnight or even a day or two to dry in the oven. Check them periodically to make sure they don't burn. If you're drying heavier leaves with a high moisture content, they should be turned over several times while drying. Tinier leaves such as thyme leaves don't require this.

A food dehydrator can also be used for drying herbs. Some people recommend using a microwave, but since you can only do a small quantity at a time in the microwave, and I always burn things in it, I prefer oven drying.

Once you've got an oven full of dried herb leaves, you may want to store the individual herbs until you're ready to actually make various blends. If so, you'll need clean glass jars. I like to pack them loosely and wait to crush the leaves (which releases the oils) until I'm actually mixing the blend or ready to cook with them.

Drying Seed

Drying and harvesting the seeds from herbs such as caraway, sesame, fennel, and dill is quite easy. As the seed-head flowers fade, you can see the seeds forming. Watch them as the seeds turn green,

and pick just as they start to turn brown. If you wait too long, you'll lose them since the dry seeds tend to fall off almost immediately. So, pick the herbs just as they're turning from green to brown, cut off the stems, hang them upside down in a brown paper bag, and tie the sack shut with the flower heads in the bag. The seeds will fall into the bag; if they don't all fall, reach into the bag with your hands and rub them off.

To harvest lavender flowers or seeds, pick either when the plant is in full bloom or just after, when it's almost a seed. I like to pick it in full bloom. Just spread the flowers out and allow to dry.

Freezing Fresh Herbs

A few of the recipes in this book recommend freezing fresh herbs, another simple preservation method. Simply combine the herbs in a blender with some water; then mix, and put into ice cube trays. These will keep in the freezer for about four months. To use them, simply pop out an ice cube or two, and throw it in the pot. Obviously this method isn't appropriate for dishes that don't have any liquid in them.

Freezing preserves more of the fresh flavor of herbs than drying does. The disadvantage is that you've got your freezer full of green ice cubes.

Blending Herbs & Spices

When you're ready to actually make your blends, decide how fine a texture you want. Some herbs and spices can simply be crushed with your fingers in a bowl and then blended well together. To preserve the best flavor, I like to coarsely crush the herbs and spices together, store them loosely packed, and then grind them more finely, if desired — in my hand or with a mortar and pestle — when I'm ready to cook with them. This allows you to save as much of the flavor as possible, making the blend finer just before eating.

I like using a mortar and pestle to crush and combine dried herbs because you can control the fineness of the texture, although the result is still somewhat coarse. For spices you probably want a smoother-textured blend. A coffee or spice grinder is nice for blending spices because most of the time you want a fine powder, and you can get that — just clean it out well before and after use if you're using a coffee grinder.

Modifying Blends & Developing Your Own

It happens to all of us. You get everything ready to make a particular herb or spice mix only to discover you're missing one of the ingredients. Most of the time I find it's better to leave it out (rather than trying to substitute something else) and just not worry — unless you're making a thyme blend and you don't have any thyme. In some cases there is a common substitute. For instance, if you were out of lemon balm, you could substitute lemon verbena, and hopefully you'd know that lemon verbena is a little stronger than lemon balm so you wouldn't use quite as much. But generally if it's not a major ingredient, I'd just leave it out. These are blends. They are meant to be adaptable and flexible, and the actual combination is often fairly arbitrary. So don't panic if you don't have one of the ingredients.

Sometimes not having one or two of the ingredients in a blend recipe inspires a new blend altogether. Often when I'm missing an ingredient, I'll substitute another herb I have on hand that I like better. Then all at once I think, oh, that would taste really good with the addition of one other herb. So the original recipe becomes a springboard for experimenting with flavors that you like — and for developing your own, new blends. Sometimes a recipe will lead to trying new herbs and spices. For instance, some of the dessert recipes in this book call for lemon- or orange-peel powder. Many people may not be used to using this ingredient. Here's a chance to try it and discover new flavor possibilities!

You can also develop your own blends of herb combinations you often use — say, for a salad dressing or a spaghetti sauce — so

you have them on hand, all mixed and ready to go. It's also very easy to develop your own mix recipes from store-bought items. Teas are a perfect example. Just go to the grocery store and check ingredient lists and ask yourself, "Why did they combine these?" Then you can pick and choose your own combination, since blending is really both unscientific and personal.

Storing Herb Mixtures & Spicy Blends

Glass containers with good, tight screw caps or corks are best for storing mixtures. They are often available at health-food stores that sell the herbs in bulk or, inexpensively, at import shops. You can also use ceramic, but you should definitely avoid aluminum. Stainless steel could be used, but most people prefer glass.

As mentioned earlier, dried herbs ideally should be used within six months, although up to one year is acceptable. After a year, flavor really starts to decline. Spices may last a little longer than herbs, but most people still keep spices in their cabinets for too long.

Finally, keep all herbs and spices in a dark place because light quickly dries up the oils. Dried herbs can also be stored in the freezer.

Packaging Your Blends

Coming up with creative packaging ideas is one of the most enjoyable parts of making your own blends. I'm one of those people who can't bear to throw away empty jars, so I've got plenty of possibilities on hand. But even if you're not a jar collector, import stores and craft-supply stores carry all kinds of wonderful and unusual containers. Just make sure the jar has a good, tight lid. If you're giving the bottled mixtures as gifts, you can add all kinds of decorative touches. Raffia comes in many different colors, and it's easy to work with. French-wired ribbon or organdy ribbon is also widely available and adds a simple elegance.

It's fun to make gift baskets by combining a bottle of herb mixture with other things. Make a gift card that gives suggestions for using the herb blend, or include a recipe card using the blend. The creators of the recipes in this book offer many suggestions. You can also make labels from purchased premade labels, from the samples in this book (on page 147), or by decorating and designing your own.

You can make presents that are very specialized for the recipient. A great Father's Day present is a basket of various blends for grilling. For somebody who enjoys baking and cooking, a basketful of three or four of the dessert blends would be wonderful. For somebody who is recovering from a heart attack, you could send a basket of no-salt blends instead of a get-well card. This is a thoughtful, practical gift.

Herb-tea blends are great to package — in mugs, teapots, or wrapped in a tea cozy. Look for empty tins at discount stores. You can really have fun fixing up these inexpensive gifts.

Think about other, related mixes to package with an herb or spice blend. With a baking blend you could include a corn bread or other specialty bread mix from a gourmet shop. Or combine a soup herb mix with a selection of colorful beans and legumes bought in bulk at a health food store and packaged in a glass jar.

All kinds of funny pasta shapes are on the market now. I've found everything from bats and baseballs to western boots and cowboy hats. A package of these combined with a jar of Italian seasoning is a great gift.

Combine a pepper/chili mix with a clear pepper mill or a bottle of herbal vinegar with a salad dressing blend. Look for crazy salt-and-pepper shakers at flea markets, antique shops, or import stores to include with a no-salt blend.

I could go on and on. Just find an appropriate size basket or fancy gift bag and you're all set. Let your imagination run wild. Herb mixtures and spicy blends are fun — and easy!

APPETIZERS, BUTTERS, AND DRESSINGS

These blend recipes for spreads, dips, dressings, butters, and cheese spreads offer lots of ideas for livening up snacks, brightening salads, and making bread and butter special. By making it yourself — from the blend to the final dish — you know exactly what you're getting, and you have the option of low-salt and low-fat alternatives. You also get a lot more flavor in your food with a homemade mix than with a ready-made one, and at less expense.

There are an infinite number of combinations you can make with herbs and cheeses. Many of the cheese and butter recipes in this chapter can be adapted to create a dip, sauce, or spread, as well. You don't have to feel bound to using the blend recipes exactly as they are given; use these as a starting place to develop your own creative uses.

Easy, low-fat alternatives to many of the butter, dip, and spread suggestions can be made by mixing the herb blend with skim milk, nonfat sour cream, or yogurt cheese (see page 3). An herb spread mixed with nonfat sour cream also makes a great dressing for cucumbers or other vegetables. Don't be afraid to experiment. After all, that's how these recipes were discovered in the first place.

Earthshine Herbal Spread Mix

*Debbie Rose Hayes of **Earthshine Herb & Book Shop** says, "I serve this blend mixed with cream cheese and spread on crackers at my workshops and special Herb Days and Open House. It has been a great success."*

YIELD: 2¾ CUPS

1 cup dried parsley
½ cup dried dillweed
½ cup dried chives
½ cup dried oregano
¼ cup dried thyme

Mix herbs thoroughly and store in an airtight container away from the light.

Variation. Add ¼ cup dried basil or ⅛ cup dried lemon zest.

Suggested Uses

 Add to cream cheese for a cracker spread.

Add to pasta sauces, dips, veggie dishes, soups and stews, salad dressings, homemade herb breads, chicken, fish dishes, herb vinegars, or herb butter.

Earthshine Herb & Book Shop
Monson, Massachusetts

Owner Debbie Rose Hayes calls Earthshine Herb & Book Shop "a veritable feast for the senses!" Visitors enter through herb and flower display gardens. A sweet-smelling mélange permeates the shop, where Debbie sells bulk herbs, spices, dried flowers, and hand-blended teas. During the growing season, she also offers fresh-cut culinary herbs and live plants. In addition, Earthshine carries aromatherapy supplies (smudges, potpourris, and fragrance and essential oils); jewelry; books on herb gardening, spirituality, and holistic health; and video and audio rentals on related subjects.

Drying Your Own Herbs

Debbie Rose Hayes recommends drying herbs by placing them on sheets or screens in the oven with a 40- to 60-watt lightbulb on. Keep the oven door ajar to allow moisture to escape. If you're lucky enough to have an older gas oven, she notes, the heat from the pilot light is great for drying herbs.

Boursin Cheese Blend

*Jan Hilty of **Herbal Lakes** offers this recipe for a classic cheese blend made with fresh herbs that can be frozen to store.*

YIELD: ABOUT ½ CUP HERB BLEND; ABOUT 1¼ POUNDS CHEESE BLEND

  2 tablespoons fresh chives
  2 tablespoons fresh parsley
1½ tablespoons fresh marjoram
  1 tablespoon fresh basil
1½ teaspoons fresh lemon thyme
  1 clove garlic
 ½ teaspoon freshly ground black pepper

Chop the herbs and garlic in a food processor; add pepper. To make spread, add ½ cup blend to 8 tablespoons softened butter (or margarine), 1 pound softened cream cheese (or light cream cheese), and whirl until blended. Chill in refrigerator for several hours. Store in freezer for up to 3 months in an airtight container. The herbs can also be stored frozen in butter; then add the cream cheese just before serving. If frozen, thaw in refrigerator, and then reblend with an electric mixer before serving.

Variation. Chop the herbs in a food processor and add enough olive oil to form a thick paste that can be stored in the refrigerator for a week to 10 days or can be frozen for 2 to 3 months. Pack paste in glass jars and cover with a layer of olive oil to prevent drying out. Use to make marinades or add to steamed vegetables, soups, and stews.

Suggested Uses

 Use cheese spread on crackers or raw vegetables.
 Warm cheese spread in a saucepan and add Parmesan cheese to taste for an Alfredo sauce to serve over pasta.

Herbal Lakes
Chagrin Falls, Ohio

Herbal Lakes owner Jan Hilty prides herself on providing personalized service, tailored to the needs of each customer. She specializes in making herbal decorations such as wreaths, garlands, and topiaries. She is also a lecturer on such topics as "Stocking Your Herbal Pantry" and is the author of a book for the Western Reserve Herb Society called *'Tis Tea Time*.

For cooks developing their own blends, Jan's advice is, "less is best when just getting started." A good way to test a blend, she says, is to mix it with butter or cottage cheese and refrigerate for 1 to 2 hours. Then spread it on a plain cracker and taste. "Remember," she adds, "your creativity is only limited by your herb garden."

Clement Herb Farm
Rogers, Arkansas

Diane Clement has been selling herbs, and educating others about the joys of herbs, from her farm in the Ozark Mountains for twenty years. The farm's products include culinary herb blends, teas, vinegars, and its very own *Clement Herb Farm Cookbook*. Diane's advice to cooks who are developing their own blends is to do lots of experimenting and tasting. "Don't forget to get all your friends to taste the finished product and offer their input," she adds.

Creamy Horseradish Spread Mix

*Diane Clement of **Clement Herb Farm** shares this spicy blend for horseradish lovers.*

YIELD: ABOUT ½ CUP HERB BLEND; 1 POUND SPREAD

    4 tablespoons dried parsley
    2 tablespoons horseradish granules or powder
    1 teaspoon garlic granules
    ½ teaspoon freshly ground black pepper

Combine all ingredients. To make a spread, add ¼ cup mixture to 16 ounces softened cream cheese and blend well. Let stand for an hour to meld flavors. May be shaped into a log or a ball and rolled in parsley. Store in airtight container in refrigerator.

Suggested Uses

 Serve spread with crudités, crackers, chips, or shrimp.
 Spread makes an excellent potato topper.
Use as a sandwich spread with roast beef.
Thin cream cheese mixture with milk to use as a dip or salad dressing.

Richland Creek Herb Mix

*Jeannie Britt of **Richland Creek Herb Farm** recommends making this recipe with fresh herbs during the growing season to appreciate the full flavor of the herbs. Just double the amount of each herb, since fresh herbs are less concentrated than dried.*

Yield: About ½ cup

    2 tablespoons dried parsley
    2 tablespoons dried oregano
    2 tablespoons dried thyme
    1 tablespoon dried cilantro

Mix herbs thoroughly and store in an airtight container away from heat and light.

Suggested Uses

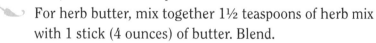

For herb cheese ball, mix together 1 tablespoon of herb mix with 8 ounces cream cheese. (For lower-fat version, use yogurt cheese, see page 3.) To form a ball, put cream cheese on plastic wrap, shape mixture into a ball, put on dish, and remove wrap.

For herb butter, mix together 1½ teaspoons of herb mix with 1 stick (4 ounces) of butter. Blend.

Richland Creek Herb Farm
Seagrove, North Carolina

The proprietors of Richland Creek Herb Farm started their business by selling plants from the back of a pickup truck, which held 48 trays of plants. As the business grew, they added shelves to the pickup, and when they outgrew that, they bought a van that carried 128 trays . . . then a second van . . . and, finally, a big box van. Today, Richland Creek Herb Farm wholesales more than 300 varieties of herbs, many of which they propagate themselves from cuttings. They have over 100 wholesale customers located in 60 towns, as well as a retail herb shop at the farm.

Making Thyme Herb Shoppe, Ltd.
Greenwood, Indiana

Proprietors Pam Herald and Laurie Meek sell bulk culinary herbs and spices in their shop, along with ready-made mixes such as the one they share here. Their other products include essential and fragrance oils, seeds, plants, books, dried floral arrangments, and dulcimer music. See their recipe for Turkey Baste on page 64.

Hoosier Party Dip Mix

*Pam Herald of **Making Thyme Herb Shoppe** submitted this Indiana favorite.*

YIELD: ABOUT 1¾ CUPS

  1 cup horseradish powder
  ½ cup dried onion flakes
  ⅓ cup dried chives

Mix ingredients thoroughly and store in airtight container.

Suggested Uses

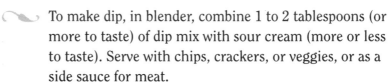 To make dip, in blender, combine 1 to 2 tablespoons (or more to taste) of dip mix with sour cream (more or less to taste). Serve with chips, crackers, or veggies, or as a side sauce for meat.

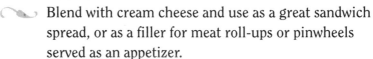 Blend with cream cheese and use as a great sandwich spread, or as a filler for meat roll-ups or pinwheels served as an appetizer.

Cream into butter. Allow to sit for several hours or overnight in fridge for full flavor. Spread on hot bread.

Hoosier Potato Salad for a Family Reunion

Pam says, "This potato salad is so good people actually think you can cook. Before taking this to a family dinner all I was ever allowed to bring was paper plates, chips, and soft drinks! So watch out; it has its pros and cons. At least it is simple to make."

YIELD: 24 SERVINGS

    4 quarts red potatoes, cooked and chopped
       with skin
    1 cup red onion, chopped
    1 cup celery, chopped
    ¾ cup relish
    6 hard-boiled eggs, chopped
    2 teaspoons celery seed
    2 or more tablespoons Hoosier Party Dip Mix
       (to taste)
    2 tablespoons Dijon-style mustard
    2 cups reduced-fat mayonnaise

Combine potatoes, onion, celery, relish, and eggs. In a separate bowl, add celery seed, dip mix, and mustard to mayonnaise. Add this to potato mixture and toss slightly. Make a day ahead for best flavor and chill before serving. Add additional mayonnaise before serving, if needed.

The Lavender Garden
Danville, Pennsylvania

The Lavender Garden is part of an antique and gift center cooperative called Cloverleaf Barn Antique & Gift Center, located in a restored Victorian barn just off Interstate Route 80. Proprietor Liz Kazio is particularly proud of the line of fourteen herbal and floral soaps she has developed that contain no mineral oil or petroleum by-products. In addition to soaps, she makes and sells herbal vinegars, honeys, potpourris, and dries and packages herbs and spices.

Winter Herb Butter Blend

*Liz Kazio of **The Lavender Garden** has both dried and fresh herb butter seasoning blends, depending on the time of year.*

YIELD: ABOUT ⅛ CUP

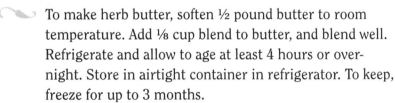

3 cloves minced garlic
3 teaspoons dried oregano
2 teaspoons dried marjoram
1 teaspoon dried thyme
½ teaspoon freshly ground black pepper
Salt to taste

Mix all ingredients thoroughly.

Suggested Uses

- To make herb butter, soften ½ pound butter to room temperature. Add ⅛ cup blend to butter, and blend well. Refrigerate and allow to age at least 4 hours or overnight. Store in airtight container in refrigerator. To keep, freeze for up to 3 months.
- Melt herb butter and use to baste poultry or add flavor to frying oil.

Summer Herb Butter Blend

The Lavender Garden's fresh herb butter blend is good on broiled fish, chicken, zucchini, or fresh sorrel soup.

YIELD: ABOUT ⅓ CUP

2–3 tablespoons dried dillweed
1 tablespoon chopped fresh parsley
2 cloves minced garlic
2 teaspoons chopped fresh lemon verbena, or
  3 drops lemon oil
½–¾ teaspoon freshly ground black pepper
  Salt to taste
  Dried mustard to taste

Mix herbs and spices thoroughly.

Suggested Use

 Soften 1 pound of butter then add ⅓ cup herb mixture. Adjust any or all seasonings to taste. Store in airtight container in refrigerator. To keep, freeze for up to 3 months.

Ladybug Press
Dallas, Texas

Lane Furneaux is Ladybug Press, a one-woman advocate for, in her own words, "how easy and enjoyable it is to grow herbs and to use them for enriching one's daily life by transforming routine tasks to meaingful adventures."

She began her activities in 1979, by convincing the owner of a Dallas grocery chain to be the first supermarket in the United States to sell freshly cut herbs, in celebration of "Herb Week." The store has stocked them ever since and, clearly, the popularity of fresh herbs has spread to supermarkets nationwide.

Lane's book, *Heavenly Herbs,* has sold nearly ten thousand copies in fifteen years and was recently released in an expanded *Love-Letters Edition,* which includes responses to readers' requests she's received through the years.

Missy's Best Blend

*Lane Furneaux of **Ladybug Press** says, "Awareness of the herbal symbolism in this mixture will surely make you try it! Thyme gives you **courage** to trust your own taste buds. Chives are very **useful**. Marjoram is the bearer of much **joy** . . . to the cook and to all tasters."*

YIELD: 1 CUP

¼ cup dried thyme
½ cup dried chives
¼ cup dried marjoram

Crush each herb well before measuring. Blend and store mixture in airtight container away from light.

Variations. Use part, or all, lemon thyme in place of thyme (good for chicken or herbal vinegar). Or add ⅛ cup garlic chives to blend.

Suggested Uses

 Stir 1½ teaspoons of best blend into 1 stick softened butter. This butter blend freezes well.

 For herb toast, spread the butter blend on bread (tiny French or sourdough loaves, or even hot dog buns) and bake slowly until tan and crisp throughout. Toast stores well for weeks in an airtight container.

 For homemade Boursin, stir 3 teaspoons of best blend into a mixture of ⅔ cup cream cheese and ⅓ cup butter; refrigerate overnight and add more blend to taste.

 Sprinkle the blend on cottage cheese, veal, or chicken.

For a superb vinaigrette dressing, combine extra-virgin olive oil with approximately ½ as much vinegar (to taste), a smidgin of sugar and/or powdered mustard, and a generous sprinkling of best blend.

Herbal Butter Mix

*Alyce Nadeau of **Goldenrod Mountain Herbs** recommends grinding this blend in small amounts in an electric coffee mill and storing unused portions away from light.*

YIELD: ABOUT ⅜ CUP

- 1 tablespoon dried chives
- 1 tablespoon dried basil
- 1 tablespoon dried parsley
- 1 tablespoon dried tarragon
- 1 tablespoon dried rosemary
- 1 tablespoon dried marjoram
- 1 teaspoon garlic powder
- ½ teaspoon lemon juice powder

Goldenrod Mountain Herbs
Deep Gap, North Carolina

Owner Alyce Nadeau grows, harvests, and crafts with herbs from her tiny farm that sits atop a ridge in the Blue Ridge Mountains. Her products include herbal wreaths, swags, vinegars, potpourris, teas, and dried herb blends. Alyce's speciality is designing herbal weddings based on the Victorian language of flowers. She also offers a "Show and Smell" tour of her herb gardens.

Mix ingredients thoroughly in order given and store in an airtight container. If lemon juice powder is unavailable, wait and add lemon juice when making the butter.

Suggested Uses

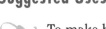 To make herbal butter, add 1 heaping teaspoon of mix to ½ pound butter or margarine that has been allowed to warm to room temperature.

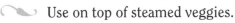 Use on top of steamed veggies.

To make herbed cream cheese, add 1 heaping teaspoon of mix to ½ pound cream cheese and blend well.

Piccadilly Herb Club
Pittsburgh, Pennsylvania

If the name of this herb club conjures up images of the old herb shops in London's Piccadilly Alley, then it's having the intended effect. Established in 1949, the club acts as a working group for the Pittsburgh Civic Garden Center and the Beechwood Audubon Center, seeking to stimulate interest in and promote knowledge of gardening with herbs.

One of the club's major activities is planning, planting, and maintaining herb, perennial, and annual gardens at the Beechwood Farms Nature Reserve. Members lead herb walks during the summer months, set up herb exhibits, and conduct plant sales. They have published a cookbook of their favorite herb recipes.

Herbed Melba Toast Blend

*One of the **Piccadilly Herb Club**'s most beloved early members was Mrs. Sidney Duerr, an educator who lectured on the flavoring qualities, healing values, and aromatic properties of herbs long before they became "trendy." She always took along a tin of Herbed Melba Toast to share with her audience. It's also good for breakfast or afternoon tea.*

YIELD: ¾ CUP

> 4 tablespoons dried thyme
> 4 tablespoons dried marjoram
> 2 tablespoons dried summer or winter savory

Mix herbs and seasonings thoroughly.

Suggested Use

 Spread room-temperature butter or margarine on slices of Pepperidge Farm Very Thin White bread. Cut each slice into 4 squares, then arrange on cookie sheet. Sprinkle each square with onion or garlic powder and the herbed blend. Bake in a 250°F oven until edges are slightly brown. Toast keeps well in an airtight refrigerated container.

Herbed Toast Mixture

Here's an alternative herbed toast recipe from the Piccadilly Herb Club's cookbook.

YIELD: ¾ CUP

    4 tablespoons dried thyme
    4 tablespoons dried marjoram
    4 tablespoons dried dillweed

Crush the herbs in a blender or food processor until very fine and place them in a jar with a shaker top.

Suggested Use

 To make toast, sauté 6–8 finely minced shallots in ½ pound lightly salted butter over very low heat, until shallots are translucent. Cut the slices from 1 loaf of Pepperidge Farm Very Thin White bread into triangles and arrange on a cookie sheet. Using a pastry brush, brush the bread with the shallot/butter mixture, trying to brush some of the shallots onto the pieces. Then lightly sprinkle the Herbed Toast Mixture over the buttered bread. Bake in a 250°F oven until toasted. Store in a refrigerated airtight container for up to 3 weeks.

Arie's Herb Gardens
Sylacauga, Alabama

Arie's Herb Gardens are located on a farm that has been in the family for five generations. The front section of the house has been converted to an herb shop. Owners Wanda Rayfield and Penny Moore recommend a strawberry jar for growing a variety of herbs, such as those used in this recipe. A different herb can be planted in each "pocket" of the jar, and they are then easily cared for and harvested. Wanda and Penny suggest keeping the jar close to the kitchen door, in a spot with plenty of sunlight.

Arie's Herb & Butter Mix

*Wanda Rayfield and Penny Moore of **Arie's Herb Gardens** distribute small samples of this mix at herb programs they present. "This whets the appetite for return business," they note.*

YIELD: ABOUT 1 CUP

- ¼ cup dried parsley
- ¼ cup dried chives
- ¼ cup dried basil
- ⅛ cup dried dillweed
- 1 tablespoon garlic powder
- 1 tablespoon dried thyme
- 1 teaspoon freshly ground black pepper

Mix all herbs and spices thoroughly and store in an airtight container away from heat and light.

Suggested Uses

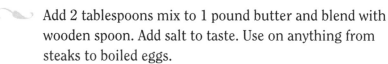 Add 2 tablespoons mix to 1 pound butter and blend with wooden spoon. Add salt to taste. Use on anything from steaks to boiled eggs.

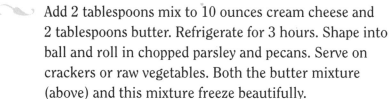 Add 2 tablespoons mix to 10 ounces cream cheese and 2 tablespoons butter. Refrigerate for 3 hours. Shape into ball and roll in chopped parsley and pecans. Serve on crackers or raw vegetables. Both the butter mixture (above) and this mixture freeze beautifully.

Green Herb Salad Dressing Mix

This recipe is for one of the Clement Herb Farm's custom blends. They make all their blends by hand, without any sugar or preservatives.

YIELD: ABOUT ½ CUP

    1   tablespoon dried chervil
    1½ teaspoons dried celery flakes
    1   teaspoon dried tarragon
    ¾   teaspoon dried basil
    ⅓   teaspoon dried dillweed
    ½   teaspoon dried thyme
    ¼   teaspoon paprika
    ⅛   teaspoon freshly ground black pepper
    ⅛   teaspoon dried garlic flakes
    1   teaspoon dried onion flakes

Mix all herbs and spices thoroughly. Store in an airtight container.

Suggested Uses

- To make salad dressing, mix herb blend with ¾ cup mayonnaise and ⅔ cup sour cream or yogurt. Place in refrigerator for several hours or overnight to blend.
- For a Green Goddess salad dressing, add 2 tablespoons anchovy paste to dressing ingredients above.

Clement Herb Farm
Rogers, Arkansas

"Education is my thing," says owner Diane Clement. From her farm on Beaver Lake in Northwest Arkansas, she has been teaching about herbs and helping others develop a passion for them for twenty years. Her business began when she approached a local nursery about selling some of her plants, since there was no local supplier at the time. Today, her business thrives by selling everything from herbal moth bags to lemon sachets and a wide range of culinary blends and bulk dried herbs.

Italian Salad Dressing Mix

Little Herb 'n Annie
Drifting, Pennsylvania

Owner Anna Marie Nachman offers herbal products for a wide range of uses, including culinary, medicinal, body care, gardening, and decorative. She also conducts in-home herbal luncheons and lectures.

*Anna Marie Nachman of **Little Herb 'n Annie** offers a homemade alternative to packaged store-bought Italian dressing mixes.*

YIELD: ABOUT ⅔ CUP

1½	tablespoons dried oregano
1½	tablespoons dried basil
1½	tablespoons garlic salt
1½	tablespoons onion powder
1½	tablespoons salt
¾	tablespoon paprika
¾	tablespoon dried dillweed
¾	tablespoon dried rosemary
½	teaspoon freshly ground black pepper
	Dash cayenne pepper

Combine all herbs and spices thoroughly.

Suggested Uses

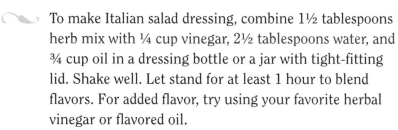 To make Italian salad dressing, combine 1½ tablespoons herb mix with ¼ cup vinegar, 2½ tablespoons water, and ¾ cup oil in a dressing bottle or a jar with tight-fitting lid. Shake well. Let stand for at least 1 hour to blend flavors. For added flavor, try using your favorite herbal vinegar or flavored oil.

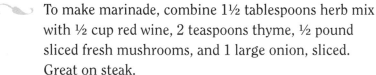 To make marinade, combine 1½ tablespoons herb mix with ½ cup red wine, 2 teaspoons thyme, ½ pound sliced fresh mushrooms, and 1 large onion, sliced. Great on steak.

Annie's Oven Roasted Potatoes

YIELD: 8 SERVINGS

8 medium potatoes
Chopped fresh chives
Chopped fresh parsley
Minced clove garlic
Salt and pepper, to taste
½ cup Little Herb 'n Annie's Italian salad dressing
(prepared as instructed at left)

Cube potatoes (washed with skins on). Place in a 13 by 9-inch baking pan. Sprinkle with chopped herbs. Add salt and pepper. Pour salad dressing over and gently stir to coat. Bake uncovered at 375°F for 1 hour, or until tender.

CHAPTER 2

MULTIPURPOSE BLENDS

T hese are the blends that you can use on practically any-thing, except maybe dessert. Throw some in an om-elette, mix some with breadcrumbs or flour to dust fish or chicken with before frying, or sprinkle some on top of pasta. These are great blends for getting into the habit of using herb mixtures. Keep a few of these mixtures on hand and you'll soon find yourself saying, "Oh, let's sprinkle a little bit of this in." These are great blends to use for giving new flavor to your old standby dishes. You really can't go wrong with a multipurpose blend.

Many of these recipes use the basic herbs most often found in an herb garden — onion, garlic, parsley, chives, rosemary, oregano, thyme, and marjoram. These are great herbs to experiment with in cooking because they can be used in a lot of different ways. Spices such as allspice and cinnamon add a bit more intense flavor that is particularly good with beans and grain, marinades, and some of the ethnic cuisines.

A few of these recipes involve freezing herb blends instead of drying — making a fresh blend into ice cubes that can be used at a later date. Frozen herbs give a lot more of the fresh flavor of herbs than dried herbs do, but there's only a finite amount of room in a freezer, so small bottles of dried blends work best for most needs.

Hillside Herb Farm
Millbach Village, Newmanstown,
Pennsylvania

Susie Iezzi's Hillside Herb Farm shop is housed in the summer house behind her 1820s Federal-style home in the quaint Pennsylvania-Dutch village of Millbach. She sells everything from potted fresh herbs to essential oils, wreaths, topiary, and freshly baked herbal breads. In addition to managing her shop, Susie also sells culinary herbs and spices, cookbooks, vinegars, redware, and breads at the Lebanon, Pennsylvania, Farmer's Market, which is held three days a week.

One of the aspects of her work Susie enjoys most is teaching about herbs — to 4-H groups, homeschoolers, young adults, and senior citizens. She's even made TV and radio appearances. Susie encourages cooks to use herbs daily, experiment, and be sure to write down your successful recipes. "I've lost a few really terrific mixes because I thought I'd remember them!" she recounts.

Iezzi's Herb Blend

*Susie Iezzi of **Hillside Herb Farm** has received rave reviews from customers for her herb blends. One couple noted that their blood pressures have dropped since they started using garlic and herbs to flavor their food. Another customer on a salt-restricted diet found his food to be blah until he began using herbs for flavoring. Garlic is great for your immune system and all-around health, notes Susie. This blend is salt-free, MSG-free, and low calorie.*

YIELD: ABOUT ¾ CUP

- 2 tablespoons dried rosemary
- 2 tablespoons dried winter savory
- 2 tablespoons garlic powder
- 2 tablespoons dried parsley
- 2 tablespoons dried chives
- 4 teaspoons onion powder
- 4 teaspoons dried oregano

Blend dried ingredients thoroughly and store in an airtight glass container away from heat and light.

Suggested Uses

 Serve on pasta, hot or cold.

 Add to omelettes, breads, oil and vinegar salad dressing, herb butter, or herb spread.

 Make an herb crust for chicken, fish, or pork, by combining 2 tablespoons herb blend with 1½ cups plain bread crumbs. (A mixture of sourdough, rye, and white bread crumbs works very nicely.) Blend together with a fork and sprinkle heavily on chicken pieces, fish fillets, or pork. Bake as usual.

All-Purpose Seasoning Blend

*Liz Kazio of **The Lavender Garden** developed this all-purpose blend that can be made with or without salt, depending on your preference.*

YIELD: 2⅓ CUPS

    5 tablespoons dried parsley
    3 tablespoons dried oregano
 2½ tablespoons dried paprika
    2 tablespoons dried celery seed
    2 teaspoons dried chile pepper
    2 tablespoons dried mustard seed
    1 tablespoon dried marjoram
    3 teaspoons dried garlic
 ½ tablespoon dried savory
    1 teaspoon dried thyme
    1 teaspoon chili powder blend
      Salt to taste (optional)

Combine all herbs and spices in a blender, spice ginder, or mortar and pestle and finely grind. Store in airtight container away from heat and light.

The Lavender Garden
Danville, Pennsylvania

Proprietor Liz Kazio has been raising herbs for eighteen years. She started The Lavender Garden in 1991 where, in addition to her retail shop, she tends a half-acre herb garden. She also consults on planning and planting gardens for other people.

Liz offers this advice on herb drying: Be sure the herbs are crispy dry before you store them. Otherwise you may get mold.

When it comes to developing blends, Liz advises starting with just two or three compatible herbs and spices, adding a little of each at a time and taste testing after each addition. Be sure to let your creation sit for one hour so the flavors meld before passing final judgment on it.

Rasland Farm
Godwin, North Carolina

Rasland Farm, a three-hundred-acre working farm that originally grew agricultural crops, began growing herbs in 1981 as an alternative crop. Today, the farm's vast herbal display and field gardens, herbal nursery, and herb shop attract visitors from around the world. Run by two generations of the Tippett family, Rasland Farm also hosts an annual Herb Fest, as well as garden tours, lectures, and demonstrations.

Chef's Delight

*Sylvia Tippett of **Rasland Farm** shares the first culinary herb blend they made fifteen years ago. "This continues to be a favorite with our customers," she says. "Some tell us it is delicious sprinkled on cheese toast, while others find it tasteful in tuna fish salad."*

YIELD: ½ CUP

- 2 tablespoons dried basil
- 1 tablespoon coarsely ground parsley
- 1 tablespoon dried chives
- 1 tablespoon dried savory
- 1 tablespoon dried marjoram
- ½ tablespoon dried lovage
- ½ tablespoon dried thyme

Mix ingredients together to blend. Store in airtight container away from heat and light.

Suggested Use

 Add to salads, soups, and meat dishes. Start by adding ½ teaspoon of the blend for a recipe that serves four people, and adjust to taste.

All-Around Spice

*Linda Laplante Beatty of **Stillwater Herb Farm** submitted this recipe that can be mixed up in nearly any quantity (using equal amounts of each ingredient) and used to spice up practically any dish.*

YIELD: ABOUT ⅔ CUP

> 2 tablespoons sesame seeds
> 2 tablespoons dried onion flakes
> 2 tablespoons garlic powder
> 2 tablespoons dried parsley
> 2 tablespoons dried thyme
>   Pinch of freshly ground black pepper

Mix ingredients thoroughly in spice jar and store away from heat and light.

Variation. Add a pinch of cayenne for extra zip.

Suggested Uses

 Use on eggs, in vegetable dishes, on chicken, and on fish.

Stillwater Herb Farm
Lewes, Delaware

Visitors can choose from over one hundred bulk herbs and spices at the Stillwater Herb Farm Country Gift Shop. Located on twenty-five acres in a beach resort town, the farm offers free tours, a display garden, nursery, and workshops on such topics as Growing Medicinals, Thyme for Tea, and Cooking Made Fun.

Stillwater Herb Farm herbalist and business partner Linda Laplante Beatty offers the following advice to cooks: "Herbs are green dynamos of vitamins, minerals, and enzymes. Add them everywhere for health, and to spice up life." She notes that "herbs and spices are like friends — some mingle well, some marry well, and some are best enjoyed separately." Linda advises keeping your mouth open while smelling an herb because then you can "taste the smell before adding it."

Thyme Remembered
Tulsa, Oklahoma

Owner Joan Stockton grows many of the herbs for the products she sells (potpourris, herbal and floral crafts, dried herbal blends, and teas) in her small backyard, which is an Oklahoma Certified Wildlife Area. Active in the Tulsa Herb Society and Garden Club, Joan encourages cooks making an all-purpose blend such as this one "to add the herbs you enjoy — and have fun with it."

Herbal Hodgepodge Blend

*Joan Stockton of **Thyme Remembered** says this is a great all-purpose blend for people who love all herbs — and just can't decide what to use. "I've included common herbs, but you can have some fun adding more exotic ones to your blend, too, such as charnushka, lemon balm, mint, orange peel, galangal, fenugreek, small amounts of chiptotle pepper, and even a touch of cinnamon and cardamom."*

YIELD: 2 CUPS

- 2 tablespoons dried basil
- 1 tablespoon dried crushed bay leaf
- 2 tablespoons dried crushed chile peppers
- 2 tablespoons dried chives
- 2 tablespoons dried ground coriander
- 2 tablespoons dried lavender leaves
- 2 tablespoons dried lemon zest
- 2 tablespoons dried marjoram
- 2 tablespoons dried oregano
- 2 tablespoons dried parsley
- 2 tablespoons dried rosemary
- 1 tablespoon dried tarragon
- 1 tablespoon dried dillweed
- 1 tablespoon dried fennel leaf (or seed)
- 1 tablespoon dried minced garlic
- 2 tablespoons dried thyme
- 1 tablespoon dried sage
- 1 tablespoon dried savory
- 1 teaspoon ground allspice
- 1 teaspoon ground ginger

Blend all the herbs thoroughly. Sprinkle allspice and ginger over the herbs, then mix again. Store in an airtight jar out of heat and light. Shake or stir before each use so herbs stay well blended.

Variation. When used for poultry, add extra tarragon. When used for pork, use blend with an equal part of rosemary. When used for salad dressing, add sesame or poppy seeds.

Suggested Uses

- Add mixture to oil and make a marinade for grilling meat or vegetables.
- Add to soups, dressings, stews, casseroles, dips, glazes, sauces (1 teaspoon for 4 servings). For a dip or other uncooked recipe, you may want to grind the blend finer in a herb grinder.

The Rosemary House, Inc.
Mechanicsburg, Pennsylvania

Founder Bertha Reppert ranks among the "pioneers" of herb-shop owners. She started The Rosemary House in 1968, in a post–Civil War row house in downtown Mechanicsburg. Bertha is proud of all they are able to produce and sell in a small space — thousands of live plants, dried herbs and spices, oils, and gifts. She made a resolution early on to develop one new product every month, and she's held true to that promise for twenty-eight years. The space outside the shop is jam-packed, as well, with display and working gardens. They hold special events in an outdoor gazebo and conduct workshops in the garage.

Rosemary's Blend

*Bertha Reppert of **The Rosemary House** says, "We are on salt-free diets, and salt is never missed with this zesty adventurous seasoning. We keep it in an acrylic peppermill so we can see the beautiful spices as we grind them on the spot."*

YIELD: VARIES, DEPENDING ON MEASUREMENT USED

- 6 parts* whole allspice berries
- 6 parts whole black peppercorns
- 3 parts whole green peppercorns
- 3 parts whole mustard seed
- 3 parts whole coriander seeds
- 2 parts fennel seeds
- 2 parts dill seeds
- 2 parts whole white peppercorns
- 1 part pine peppercorns (optional)
- 1 part whole dried chile peppers

* "Parts" can be translated into teaspoons, tablespoons, or cups for a larger quantity.

Mix all of these colorful whole spices and store in an airtight jar away from heat and light. Use a peppermill to enjoy them freshly ground.

Variation. Add pretty pink whole dried rosebuds for an unexpected flavor.

Suggested Uses

 Grind onto bland veggies such as stewed squash.
Add to Middle Eastern or Asian dishes, chicken recipes, and stews.
 Use on eggs dishes.

Arie's Herb Salt

*Wanda Rayfield and Penny Moore of **Arie's Herb Gardens** developed this recipe for improving on salt.*

YIELD: 1 CUP

10	tablespoons salt
5	tablespoons white pepper
1	teaspoon ground nutmeg
1	teaspoon ground cloves
1	teaspoon ground cinnamon
1	teaspoon dried crushed bay leaf
1	teaspoon dried sage
1	teaspoon dried parsley
1	teaspoon dried rosemary

Finely grind all ingredients. Blend well and package in airtight containers. Store away from heat and light.

Suggested Use

 For flavoring baked chicken, combine herb salt with ½ cup soy sauce and ½ cup dry sherry; add during last 15 minutes of baking.

Arie's Herb Gardens
Sylacauga, Alabama

As part of their effort to educate people about herbs, partners Wanda Rayfield and Penny Moore present programs geared to the interests of individual audiences. These have included: Herbs of Christmas (for several civic groups), Herbs of the Bible (for church groups), Growing Herbs (for garden clubs), and Herbs in Colonial America (for fifth-grade social studies classes).

For cooks experimenting with developing herb blends, Wanda and Penny recommend trying out various combinations on your family or supper club. And, they remind you, be patient until you come up with just the right combination.

Devonshire Apothecary
Austin, Texas

For the past ten years, Devonshire Apothecary has toured Renaissance festivals and craft fairs across the country, selling its tinctures, botanicals, spice blends, culinary and medicinal herbs, bath herbs, essential oils, and handmade incense. These activities have spawned a mail-order and wholesale business with over two hundred customers all over the world, from Canada to Japan. In 1994, the company opened a retail store in one of the older ethnic neighborhoods of Austin. Here, amid small shops and restaurants, Devonshire Apothecary has found a place to establish a small herb garden and sell its growing range of products.

Devonshire Apothecary Seasoning Base

*The kitchen herbs used in this recipe from **Devonshire Apothecary** are effective in aiding digestion. Asafetida by itself smells horrible, but it is a wonderful herb when used in combination with others.*

YIELD: ABOUT 1⅓ CUPS

    8 teaspoons kelp powder
    7 teaspoons granulated garlic
    7 teaspoons dried basil
    6 teaspoons celery seeds, whole
    4 teaspoons black ground pepper
    4 teaspoons onion flakes or powder
    3 teaspoons Hungarian paprika
    3 teaspoons dried marjoram
    3 teaspoons dried rosemary
    2 teaspoons tumeric powder
    2 teaspoons dried Greek oregano
    2 teaspoons dried parsley
    2 teaspoons coriander seeds, whole
    2 teaspoons dried tarragon
    2 teaspoons dried thyme
    2 teaspoons dried savory
    1 teaspoon caraway seed, whole
    1 teaspoon dried dillweed
    1 teaspoon cumin seed, whole
    1 teaspoon dried sage
    1 teaspoon dried bay leaf, whole
    1 teaspoon asafetida powder

Mix all herbs and spices thoroughly and store in airtight container away from heat and light.

Variation. Add several sea vegetables to transform this seasoning base into a good salt substitute.

Suggested Uses

 This blend is excellent in soups, or sprinkled on fish or vegetables before broiling. It nicely spices tofu cubes for veggie kabobs, too.

Not Salt

YIELD: ABOUT ¾ CUP

>   6 tablespoons dried dulse seaweed, whole
>   3 tablespoons kelp powder
>   2 tablespoons dried Irish moss
>   2 tablespoons Devonshire Apothecary
>   Seasoning Base

Grind up ingredients and use liberally.

The Rosemary House's "Les Fines Herbes" Seasoning

*This is **The Rosemary House's** version of a traditional blend that usually includes a mixture of some of the following herbs: chives, parsley, chervil, thyme, savory, tarragon, sweet marjoram, and oregano.*

Yield: ½ cup

6	tablespoons dried chervil
1	tablespoon dried sweet basil
1	tablespoon dried tarragon
1	teaspoon dried sweet marjoram
½	teaspoon dried thyme
½	teaspoon dried rosemary

Mix thoroughly, grind as finely as possible (in a food processor, if you like), and store in an airtight jar. Use sparingly.

Suggested Uses

 Add Les Fines Herbes to chowders a few minutes before serving. Use on vegetables just as serving. Use in any egg dish or cheese casserole.

United Society of Shakers Fish and Egg

This recipe has been used in every Shaker cookbook ever published and is a favorite of the Shaker family at Sabbathday Lake. About thirty years ago it was considered a rather economical dish, especially when the community had its own dairy herd. The cream and butter were plentiful then, and a pound of salt codfish cost only 39 cents. This dish was made for the Shaker family when it numbered sixty people and was made in huge double boilers.

YIELD: 6 SERVINGS

- 2 cups whole milk or light cream
- 1 tablespoon butter or margarine
- 3 boiled potatoes, chilled and sliced thinly
- 1 cup codfish, boiled and shredded
- 6 hard-boiled eggs, sliced
- ¼ teaspoon salt
- Dash of pepper
- ½ teaspoon Les Fines Herbes

Scald milk and add butter. In a buttered baking dish, place a layer of boiled potatoes, then a layer of codfish, and then a layer of eggs. Repeat until the dish is filled. Add seasonings. Cover with hot milk. With a knife or spoon, allow milk to seep down through mixture. Bake at 325°F for 50 minutes until milk has been absorbed. Garnish top with parsley.

United Society of Shakers
**Sabbathday Lake
New Gloucester, Maine**

Long before today's herb craze, the Shakers were growing and using herbs in medicine and cooking. The Shaker community at Sabbathday Lake has been selling culinary herbs, teas, and their own specialty blends since 1799. The herbs are all raised organically in the community gardens. The traditional Shaker recipe "Fish and Egg" uses the classic herb seasoning "Les Fines Herbes," as formulated by The Rosemary House.

Becker's Cottage Garden
Herb Farm
Akron, Ohio

Jan Becker's herb business truly grew out of her own garden, when friends and neighbors asked if she would grow a few extra herbs for them. Even today, she says, "It doesn't feel like a business. It just feels like we're enjoying our herbs, and sharing our plants and ideas with friends." The business's growth has been solely through word-of-mouth.

Jan has her own blend-developing technique that she passes on to others. "I blend things in percentages, according to how well I like each herb or spice on its own. The more I like it, the higher the percentage of it that goes into the blend."

Becker's Freezer Herbs

Jan Becker of Becker's Cottage Garden Herb Farm says this all-purpose freezer blend seems to work for everything.

YIELD: APPROXIMATELY 6 FROZEN CUBES

½ cup fresh basil
1 tablespoon fresh marjoram
1 tablespoon fresh thyme
1 tablespoon fresh rosemary
1 tablespoon fresh savory
1 tablespoon fresh oregano
¼ cup olive oil

Chop the leaves of the herbs and combine in blender with the olive oil. Pour into ice cube trays and freeze.

Suggested Uses

 Thaw cubes in microwave. Combine several cubes with ½ cup freshly grated Parmesan cheese and add to a basic muffin recipe for great herbed muffins. Or combine a few cubes with melted butter and finely chopped or roasted garlic and spread on crusty bread.

 Combine several thawed cubes with melted butter and salt to pour over popcorn. Or use several cubes to season spaghetti sauce.

All-Purpose Vegetable Seasoning

*Lucinda Lux of **Secret Garden Herb Shoppe** began experimenting with all-purpose blends when she got tired of having to root through all her herb and spice jars, especially when she was in a hurry. This is one of the recipes she came up with.*

YIELD: ABOUT ½ CUP

> 2 tablespoons dried oregano
> 2 tablespoons dried thyme
> 2 tablespoons dried basil
> 1 tablespoon dried marjoram
> ½ tablespoon dried rubbed sage

Mix all ingredients together and store in airtight glass container.

Suggested Uses

- Sprinkle seasoning on cooked and steamed vegetables. Add a dab of butter, onion and/or garlic powder, and lemon zest.
- Add seasoning to casseroles and goulash dishes.

Secret Garden Herb Shoppe
Springville, New York

Owner Lucinda Lux started the Secret Garden Herb Shoppe in 1993 after the seasonal herb farm she had been working for moved out of state. "I couldn't bear not to be working with herbs," she recounts. Over time, she's expanded the scope of her shop to include everything from herb seasonings, potpourris, and herbal health-care products to Native American leather footware, mandalas, smudge herbs, and leather pouches. "I call it my New Age herb shop," she says.

CHAPTER 3

No-Salt Blends

erb blends are quickly taking the place of the salt shaker on the kitchen table. With increased health warnings about the dangers of high-sodium diets, many people are looking for other ways to make food savory. The recipes in this chapter offer a good variety of easy-to-make, salt-free seasoning alternatives.

Many of the multipurpose blends in Chapter 2 are also salt-free, but the recipes in this chapter have been created especially to be used in place of salt, as you would generally use salt. Many of these blends are finely ground, so they can be placed is some kind of shaker bottle.

If you are on a salt-free diet, you should be aware of the fact that a couple of these recipes use sea vegetables (such as dulse and kelp), which do contain sodium chloride. The amount of sodium chloride in the total recipe, however, is much less than that of straight salt, and sea vegetables contain a lot of valuable trace minerals, as well, which give them other beneficial properties.

Kathleen Gips' Village Herb
Shop/Pine Creek Herbs
Chagrin Falls, Ohio

Kathleen Gips was enticed into the herb world by a fascination with tussie mussies and the language of flowers. Tussie mussies — small, tightly gathered, handheld bouquets of herbs and flowers — have held symbolic and practical importance throughout history, beginning in the Middle Ages when both men and women carried them to ward off disease and disguise unpleasant odors. Today, the bouquets are made with careful attention to the symbolism of each flower and herb used. Kathleen has written books on this, and offers a variety of tussie mussies in her shop and through her mail-order catalog.

Kathleen also offers a line of herb blends, named for the types of food they best complement. She shares her best-selling blend here.

Salt-Free Herb Salt

*Kathleen Gips at the **Village Herb Shop** suggests using petite basil and savory to make this mixture easy to shake from a wide-holed shaking jar.*

YIELD: ABOUT ⅔ CUP

- 2 tablespoons dried basil
- 2 tablespoons dried parsley
- 2 tablespoons dried marjoram
- 2 tablespoons dried savory
- 2 teaspoons ground rosemary
- 2 teaspoons sweet paprika
- 2 teaspoons onion granules (not powder)
- 2 teaspoons powdered milk (aids shaking and prevents caking)

Mix ingredients together thoroughly to blend and keep in an airtight container away from heat and light.

Herbal Unsalt

*This salt substitute comes from **Rainbow's End Herbs**.*

YIELD: ABOUT ¾ CUP

 3 tablespoons dried basil
 2 tablespoons dried savory
 2 tablespoons celery seed
1½ tablespoons dried sage
 1 tablespoon dried thyme
 1 teaspoon powdered kelp
 1 tablespoon dried marjoram

Powder the herbs in a spice grinder or blender. Transfer to a shaker when well blended. Set alongside the salt and pepper at the table.

Suggested Use

 Delicious in soups and stews, and on eggs, beans, and meats. Adds great flavor to bland or low-salt diets.

Rainbow's End Herbs
Perrysburg, New York

Jacqueline Swift has been producing medicinal, edible, and fragrant herb products since 1978 in the wine country of western New York State.

For cooks growing their own basil for this recipe, Jacqueline says, "I direct-seed basil in early May, cover with burlap until the seeds sprout, and then protect them from frost as needed. Basil plants look beautiful grown in short rows across a four-foot bed. Make a border of spicy globe basil plants."

No-Salt Sesame Seasoning

Walk In Beauty
Colfax, California

Kathy Lee operates her mail-order herb business from a historic railroad town in the Sierra Nevada foothills. She also travels extensively, teaching herb classes and workshops. Kathy began the business in 1991 as a way of pursuing her interests in the healing arts and creative cooking. She is particularly intrigued by how to incorporate nutrient-rich herbs and spices that have medicinal properties into cooking. In this recipe, she uses seaweeds with high nutritional value.

Kathy Lee of **Walk In Beauty** *notes that dulse, hijiki, and kelp are all seaweeds, which are very rich in flavor and loaded with nutritional benefits. Dulse is high in iron and protein as well as many other vitamins and trace minerals, including calcium. This easy recipe makes a tasty high-calcium condiment for healthier meals.*

YIELD: ABOUT 1⅔ CUPS

- 1 cup sesame seeds
- 1 tablespoon garlic powder
- 1 tablespoon dulse flakes
- 1 tablespoon celery seed
- 1 tablespoon dried alfalfa
- 1 tablespoon dried parsley

Roast sesame seeds in a heavy pan over medium heat, stirring constantly to prevent burning. When lightly browned, pour into blender or food processor and add all other ingredients. Grind to desired texture.

Variation. If you can't find dulse flakes, use an equal amount of hijiki (ground) or a pinch of kelp powder.

Suggested Uses

 This seasoning is excellent on salads, steamed greens, and even on vegetables and in casseroles.

Sweet Remembrances Salt-Free Blend

Nancy Reppert of Sweet Remembrances centers her tables with a pretty bunch of herbs, a salt shaker, peppermill, and a shaker of this salt-free blend for flavorful seasonings.

YIELD: 1⅓ CUPS

> 6 tablespoons dried parsley
> 4 tablespoons dried oregano
> 4 tablespoons onion powder
> 2 tablespoons dried basil
> 2 teaspoons garlic powder
> 1 teaspoon dried rosemary
> 1 teaspoon dried thyme
> 1 teaspoon dried sage
> ½ teaspoon cayenne powder
> 1 tablespoon dried safflower petals (optional), to impart a golden color to blend

Grind all dried herbs thoroughly in a grinder or blender and put in a large-holed shaker.

Variation. This blend can be mixed half and half with salt for a salt taste with a considerable reduction in salt intake.

Suggested Uses

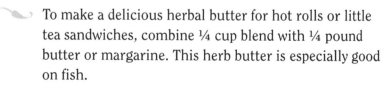

To make a delicious herbal butter for hot rolls or little tea sandwiches, combine ¼ cup blend with ¼ pound butter or margarine. This herb butter is especially good on fish.

This is a general seasoning suitable for meat, fish, chicken, salads, and vegetables.

Sweet Remembrances
Mechanicsburg, Pennsylvania

Having grown up working in her mother's herb shop, The Rosemary House, Nancy Reppert's love of herbs has deep roots. She didn't have to move far from home to pursue her own dreams — Sweet Remembrances, "a private party place" offering afternoon herbal tea and special-occasion catering, is right next door to The Rosemary House. Nancy's specialties are edible flowers and sinful desserts. Her salt-free blend might help counteract some of the effects of her irresistable cakes.

The Rosemary House
Mechanicsburg, Pennsylvania

Bertha Reppert has been experimenting with no-salt herb blends for fifteen years, since she and her husband embarked on salt-free diets. She generously shared several of the salt-free blend recipes that they give out to customers at The Rosemary House. Bertha encourages cooks to experiment with these blends, to avoid having the same flavor at every meal.

For herb growers, Bertha advises "Keep them clipped!" Regular clipping keeps herb plants healthy and productive. Her drying method consists of putting the herbs in the oven on cookie sheets, at 150°F for 30 minutes before using them in blends. Leave the oven door slightly ajar to allow moisture to escape.

Better-Than-Salt Herb Blend

Yield: 1 cup

3 dried bay leaves, broken up
4 tablespoons dried oregano leaves
4 tablespoons onion powder
1 tablespoon dried lemon zest*
4 teaspoons dried marjoram
4 teaspoons dried basil
4 teaspoons ground dried savory, preferably winter savory
4 teaspoons garlic powder
2 teaspoons dried rosemary
1 teaspoon dried sage
1 teaspoon dried thyme leaves
1 teaspoon ground black pepper

* Lemon zest is the yellow peel without the white pith. A potato peeler does the job nicely on a firm lemon. Slice thinly and dry before mixing.

Mix the herbs and crush to a coarse powder with a mortar and pestle, or put through an electric coffee mill to reduce finely enough to put into a large-holed shaker. Store extra in an airtight container.

Variation. Mix this blend with a stick of butter or margarine. Let stand in the refrigerator for a day or two for best flavor, then use on vegetables, breads, meats, and fish.

Suggested Uses

 Delicious on salad greens, on sliced tomatoes and cucumbers, on fish, hamburgers, meat loaves, steaks, and omelettes.

Saltless Herb Salt

YIELD: ⅔ CUP

- 3 tablespoons dried basil
- 2 tablespoons celery seed
- 2 tablespoons dried savory
- 1½ tablespoons sage
- 1 tablespoon dried thyme
- 1 tablespoon dried marjoram
- 1 teaspoon dried kelp
- ½ teaspoon dried sassafras leaves

Mix the ingredients and crush to a coarse powder using a mortar and pestle. Keep in an airtight container.

Suggested Use

 Use in soups, stews, or rice.

Saltless Salt for Chicken

YIELD: VARIES

- 2 parts dried rosemary
- 1 part dried thyme
- 1 part dried marjoram
- 1 part dried savory
- 1 part dried basil

Mix the herbs and grind finely.

Suggested Use

 Rub on chicken for roasting, frying, or grilling.

Woodland No-Salt Herb Blend

Woodland Herb Gardens
Spicer, Minnesota

Woodland Herb Gardens grows herbs and display gardens on two lakeshore acres in western Minnesota. They use no pesticides or chemicals, and note that their herbs have a wonderful flavor since there's no need to worry about the oils being baked out of them in Minnesota's cool weather!

Owner Javis Jante says that when they started their gardens in 1991, she had never cooked with herbs. In response to customer requests, she mixed up her first herb blend — simply by combining the twelve herbs she had dried that year with some garlic and onion powder. After a bit more experimenting, and taste testing by visitors, this blend has become one of their popular standards.

*Jarvis Jante, of **Woodland Herb Gardens**, says, "When we started our gardens five years ago, I was not using herbs and did not know how to use them in cooking. Knowing I would have to learn quickly, I mixed all our herbs together and started experimenting, with this result."*

YIELD: ABOUT 1 CUP

- 4 tablespoons onion powder
- 4 teaspoons dried winter savory
- 4 teaspoons dried marjoram
- 4 teaspoons garlic powder
- 4 tablespoons dried oregano
- 4 teaspoons dried basil
- 2 bay leaves, finely chopped
- 2 teaspoons dried rosemary
- 2 teaspoons dried tarragon
- 1 teaspoon dried thyme
- 1 teaspoon dried sage

Blend all ingredients in a small food processor and grind well. If you grow and dry your own herbs, the flavor will be far superior to that of purchased dried herbs.

Variation. Using most of the basic herbs, you can add chervil, parsley, or chives with good results.

Suggested Uses

 Use on anything but dessert! Soups, salads, vegetables, popcorn, sprinkled on meat before grilling, mixed with hamburger for meatloaf, meatballs.

Dry Creek Herb Farm Popcorn Seasoning

*Shatoiya de la Tour, of **Dry Creek Herb Farm and Learning Center**, says, "Many of my customers are happy that their children love this healthful seasoning on popcorn. The nutritional yeast is an excellent source of the B vitamins. The kelp is blood building, and the herbs aid digestion."*

YIELD: ABOUT 5 CUPS

- ½ cup dried marjoram
- ½ cup dried thyme
- ½ cup dried basil
- 2 cups cheddar cheese powder
- 1 cup nutritional yeast powder
- ½ cup garlic powder
- ¼ cup kelp powder

In a spice grinder, powder the marjoram, thyme, and basil. Mix well with the rest of the ingredients. Store in an airtight glass container away from heat and light.

Variation. Mixture may also be used with oil and vinegar as a salad dressing.

Suggested Use

 Sprinkle liberally on lightly buttered popcorn.

Dry Creek Herb Farm and Learning Center
Auburn, California

Owners Shatoiya and Rick de la Tour are proud of their organic herb gardens, where many visitors come to find peace and learn about herbs. They place a heavy emphasis on the benefits of organically grown herbs, and offer the following advice for growing the herbs used in their popcorn seasoning: "Thyme likes abuse. It can grow in poor soil with little water. Many people kill their thyme by overwatering it. It's best to harvest it for drying just as the blossoms begin to form. Marjoram is an easy-to-grow, tender perennial. Besides cooking with it, we blend it with lavender to make headache pillows and add it to the bath for smooth skin."

JoHanna's Cellar Babies
Youngstown, Ohio

Owner JoAnne Fajack's specialty is making folk-art dolls incorporating herbs. Her doll named Herbal Delight is made from muslin and old quilts with wings of sweet Annie, sage, artemesia, or silver king. She is planted in a pot carrying rosemary. In addition to her dolls, JoAnne offers herbal arrangements, vinegars, oils, and sachets.

JoHanna's Salt Substitute

*JoAnne Fajack, of **JoHanna's Cellar Babies**, developed this recipe after her husband had a heart attack and salt was taken out of his diet. "This mixture gives meats the taste of salt, except it is a lot better for you," says JoAnne. "The paprika gives it a pretty color, but the other herbs give it the great flavor."*

YIELD: ABOUT ½ CUP

    2 tablespoons onion powder
    2 tablespoons garlic powder
    2 tablespoons Italian seasoning
    2 teaspoons dried tarragon
    2 teaspoons dried oregano
    2 teaspoons parsley flakes
    2 teaspoons paprika

Combine all ingredients and mix well. Place in a wide-hole shaker jar to use at the table in place of salt.

Variation. Crushed-up bay leaves can be substituted for tarragon.

Suggested Uses

 Great on steak, pork chops, beef patties, and especially in chicken dishes. This blend is very mild and yet tasteful.

Kate's Savory Seasoning

*Kate Warden of **Herbal Essence** says this recipe can be used in any dish calling for a ground seasoning.*

YIELD: ABOUT ¾ CUP

- 3 tablespoons dried marjoram, ground
- 3 tablespoons dried savory, ground
- 2 tablespoons dried thyme, ground
- 2 tablespoons garlic powder
- 2 tablespoons kelp powder
- 1 tablespoon dried basil, ground
- ⅓ tablespoon cayenne powder

Mix ingredients together thoroughly to blend and store in an airtight container away from heat and light.

Variation. Add 2½ tablespoons dried lemon peel.

Suggested Uses

 Great on popcorn, steamed veggies, and any pasta.
 Use in place of poultry seasoning or salt and pepper.

Herbal Essence
Scottsdale, Arizona

Kate Warden specializes in herbal medicinals, original seasonings, teas, and potpourris.

CHAPTER 4

MEAT AND SEAFOOD SEASONINGS

Meat and seafood seasonings can easily transform a simple dish into an unusual dish. There's something here for everyone — from light dillweed and lemon balm seasonings for fish and chicken to stronger-tasting blends with juniper berries for wild game and duck.

The meat seasonings are versatile. You can sprinkle the herb mixture directly on the meat, add it to breadcrumbs for coating before frying or baking, or blend it with oil, vinegar, or shoyu to make a marinade or basting sauce.

Poultry seasonings can be sprinkled directly on the meat, added to a chicken or turkey casserole, or mixed in with the stuffing. If you're leaving the skin on the bird, rub the herb mixture under the skin before roasting. A basting mixture can also be made by adding the herb and spice blend to orange juice. Lemon juice and white wine make a nice glazing baste.

The seafood blends also offer lots of options, from sprinkling the herbs on or in a whole fish for sautéing or baking to incorporating the blend into a sauce to use after baking. Many of the seafood blends would work nicely in a potato soup or cream-based soup as well. They can also be more finely ground for use at the table.

The Secret Garden Herb Shoppe
Springville, New York

In addition to running her herb shop, owner Lucinda Lux offers herbal cooking classes held at the local high school in the evenings. She advises cooks experimenting with blends to make "mini-batches" first, blending them with a bit of butter or cottage cheese (something bland) to taste test. Be sure to write down the amounts so they can be expanded later if it turns out to be a blend you like. Lucinda also notes that "freshly dried is always best," and being able to say "I grew and dried the herbs myself" gives great satisfaction.

All-Purpose Meat Seasoning

*Lucinda Lux, of **The Secret Garden Herb Shoppe**, developed this all-purpose blend for seasoning all kinds of meats and poultry.*

2 parts rubbed sage
2 parts dried marjoram
1 part dried oregano
1 part dried thyme
1 part dried basil
1 part dried rosemary
1 part dried savory
½ part dried French tarragon
3 parts crumbled bay leaf

Mix all ingredients together and store in an airtight glass container. Sprinkle on meat or poultry along with onion and garlic powder before roasting or broiling. Discard bay leaf pieces before eating. Do not consume bay leaves!

Quatre Épices (Four Spices)

*Bertha Reppert, of **The Rosemary House,** shares this recipe for a salt-free version of a classic meat seasoning with participants in her cooking class.*

YIELD: ABOUT ⅔ CUP

> 5 tablespoons freshly ground pepper, black or white
> 2 tablespoons cayenne powder
> 2 tablespoons ground ginger
> 1 tablespoon ground cloves

Mix ingredients together thoroughly to blend.

Suggested Use

Use on meats and pâtés.

The Rosemary House
Mechanicsburg, Pennsylvania

Bertha Reppert, who founded The Rosemary House in 1968, has been a mentor and friend to many more recent herb shops and businesses. She shares many of her tips for herb business owners in her book *Growing Your Herb Business* (Storey Publishing, 1994). While retired from running the daily shop, Bertha continues to offer classes at The Rosemary House, which is now run by her daughter Susanna.

Herb Blend for Lamb

*This blend of favorite lamb seasonings comes from Mary Reeve of **Hilltop Herbery**.*

YIELD: 1½ CUPS

- ½ cup dried rosemary
- ½ cup dried mint, crumbled
- ¼ cup dried summer savory
- ⅛ cup dried thyme
- ⅛ cup dried marjoram
- 2 tablespoons dried parsley

Combine all ingredients thoroughly. Store in airtight container in a dark place away from heat.

Suggested Use

 Use to season all cuts of lamb and lamb dishes.

Hilltop Herbery
Cazenovia, New York

From her farm in the rolling hills of central New York State, Mary Reeve enjoys working with gourmet chefs at many of the area inns who are creative in using herbs and edible flowers in their cooking. Herbs have opened up all kinds of opportunities for Mary, from providing Native Americans with herbs for ritual celebrations to supplying fresh herbs for a gourmet supermarket to sharing herbs with others through classes.

Poultry Seasoning

*This is another specialty seasoning from **Hilltop Herbery** that makes a great gift. Try packaging it in a small jar or colorful cellophane bag.*

YIELD: 4½ CUPS

   2 cups dried parsley
   1 cup dried sage, crumbled
  ½ cup dried summer savory
  ½ cup dried rosemary
  ¼ cup dried lovage
  ¼ cup dried marjoram
   1 teaspoon freshly ground black pepper
   1 teaspoon dried onion powder

Combine herbs and seasonings thoroughly, and store in airtight container in a dark place away from heat.

Suggested Use

 Use for seasoning all poultry, casseroles, and stuffing.

Randallane Chicken Seasoning

This homemade shake and bake mixture is from Judith Graves of Lambs & Thyme at Randallane.

YIELD: 1½ CUPS

1	teaspoon salt
1	teaspoon paprika
1	teaspoon garlic salt
½	teaspoon celery salt
½	teaspoon ground black pepper
⅛	teaspoon ground ginger
⅛	teaspoon dried thyme
⅛	teaspoon dried oregano
1	cup flour
½	cup cornmeal

Combine all ingredients, mix well, and store in airtight container.

Suggested Use

 For fried chicken, place herb mixture in a brown paper bag. Shake boneless, skinless chicken breasts in the mixture until well coated. Preheat oven to 350°F. Fry in canola oil in large skillet just until brown then place chicken in an uncovered baking dish. Bake in oven for 20 minutes.

Lambs & Thyme at Randallane
Richmond, New Hampshire

The gardens of Lambs & Thyme spread out over the countryside of the sixty-five-acre homestead of David and Judith Graves. Their home dates back to 1763, the oldest recorded in the town of Richmond, New Hampshire, and was built by Abraham Randall. A small lane that runs near the house, which led to two brickyards in the 1700s, came to be known as "Randallane."

Today, visitors can take part in workshops, garden teas (including special Victorian-theme teas), tours, and an annual herb festival. They can also shop for antiques, herbal culinaries, crafts, remedies, dried flowers, and folk art in an 1855 schoolhouse that was reconstructed on the property in 1993.

Randallane Fish & Herbs

Lambs & Thyme at Randallane developed this blend especially for fish dishes. Judith Graves says, "When looking for a blend to go with a particular food, do your homework and fully explore what each herb has to offer. Herbs open a wide world to our taste buds."

YIELD: ABOUT ⅓ CUP

    8 teaspoons dried onion flakes
    4 teaspoons dried rosemary or dried tarragon
    4 teaspoons dried parsley
  ¼ teaspoon ground black pepper
  ¼ teaspoon paprika

Mix all ingredients and store in airtight jar until ready to use.

Suggested Use

 Sprinkle to taste over fish before baking, broiling, or grilling.

Herb Shoppe Turkey Baste Blend

Making Thyme Herb Shoppe, Ltd.
Greenwood, Indiana

In addition to the retail sales they conduct at Making Thyme Herb Shoppe, owners Pam Herald and Laurie Meek also offer classes on such topics as: Now that I've grown it, what do I do with it? and Biblical Herbs. They publish a quarterly newsletter, as well.

*This is one of many specialty herb blends Pam Herald and Laurie Meek of **Making Thyme Herb Shoppe, Ltd.** have developed. The low-fat turkey baste is great for Thanksgiving and Christmas, but don't reserve it only for holidays.*

YIELD: ABOUT ½ CUP

1½ teaspoons dried thyme
  3 tablespoons dried sage
  2 tablespoons dried parsley
  1 tablespoon ground fennel seed
  1 tablespoon ground white pepper
  ¾ teaspoon nutmeg
  ¾ teaspoon allspice
  ¾ teaspoon dry yellow mustard
  ¾ teaspoon dried chervil
  ¾ teaspoon dried savory

Combine all 10 herbs thoroughly and store in airtight container.

Suggested Uses

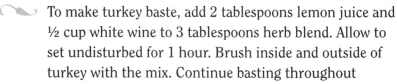

To make turkey baste, add 2 tablespoons lemon juice and ½ cup white wine to 3 tablespoons herb blend. Allow to set undisturbed for 1 hour. Brush inside and outside of turkey with the mix. Continue basting throughout cooking.

For sandwiches or salads, cook turkey or chicken with baste, and then slice thinly.

Fowl and Fish Blend

*Theresa Briere of **Broadacres Herbs** says, "I have used this recipe to flavor wild mushrooms (cultivated ones also work well) stewed in olive oil and apple cider vinegar, which makes a great side dish to accompany wild game meals, or a condiment. Sometimes the simplest herb blends are the most effective ones!"*

YIELD: ABOUT ½ CUP

- ¼ cup dried dillweed
- 2 tablespoons dried lemon balm
- 1 tablespoon garlic granules

Combine herbs and store in airtight jar away from light and heat.

Variation. Leave out the garlic if delicately flavored fish is desired. Lemongrass or lemon basil can be substituted for lemon balm.

Suggested Uses

- Use to season fish or fowl dishes, in a marinade, or in stuffing, gravy, or a cream sauce for fish or fishcakes, vegetables, roasted potatoes, or potato soup.
- Wonderful on fresh sliced tomatoes and cucumbers with a dressing of mayonnaise diluted with a little apple cider vinegar.

Broadacres Herbs
South China, Maine

Co-owner Theresa Briere uses organically grown or wild-crafted herbs to craft herb blends for all kinds of culinary and nonedible uses. Her creations include teas, pet care, insect repellent, tinctures, pillow blends, salves, lip balms, bath and body care products, and wild foods.

Cricket Hill Herb Farm
Rowley, Massachusetts

Located on a quiet country road —
yet easily accessible from major
highways — on Boston's North Shore,
Cricket Hill Herb Farm is particularly
appreciated for its setting. As owner
Judith Kehs describes it, "Our
greenhouses and display gardens are
bounded on one side by a hedgerow
sheltering a variety of birdlife (and the
inevitable groundhogs and bunnies)
and on the other side by rolling fields
that blend into forested areas and
marshlands along Rowley's Mill River.
Our location is both spectacular and
peaceful."

All-Purpose Fish/Seafood Seasoning

*Judy Kehs of **Cricket Hill Herb Farm** says that most of
her own blends grew out of years of experiments, with
many failures as well as successes. "Never make the
mistake of assuming that if a little of a certain herb
tastes good in a dish, a lot more of that herb will
make it much better," Judy cautions. "Increase herb
amounts gradually and taste test judiciously. Too
much tarragon, for instance, puckers your lips and
tongue and makes for an unpleasant culinary
experience!"*

YIELD: ABOUT ⅔ CUP

    2 tablespoons dried tarragon
    2 tablespoons dried basil
    2 tablespoons dried marjoram
    2 tablespoons dried chervil
    2 tablespoons dried parsley

Combine all ingredients and store in an airtight container.

Suggested Uses

 Use on baked, broiled, grilled, or even fried fish (add to
the batter).

 Mix with butter and bread crumbs for breading on fish or
shellfish.

 Add seasoning to soups and chowders.

Customer's Choice Seafood Seasoning

*One of **Cricket Hill Herb Farm's** customers developed this savory blend that enhances seafood, especially shellfish dishes.*

YIELD: ABOUT 1 CUP

    4 tablespoons sea salt (optional)
    4 tablespoons celery seed
    2 tablespoons mustard seed or ground dry mustard
    2 tablespoons dried thyme*
    1 tablespoon ground ginger
   ½ tablespoon dried green peppercorns
   ¼ tablespoon white peppercorns
   ⅛ tablespoon allspice berries or ground allspice
   ⅛ tablespoon crushed bay leaf

*Lemon thyme is even better.

Combine all ingredients and process in a food mill or spice grinder until coarsely ground. Salt helps in the grinding process, but if you are trying to cut back, use just a small amount.

Suggested Use

 Blend this seasoning with melted butter and use to top broiled fish, especially swordfish steaks.

Louise Downey — Herbalist
Bethel, Vermont

Louise Downey has used her seafood seasoning recipe as the basis of a talk on "creating your own personal herb blend" that she has presented at the Boston Flower Show and to various garden clubs. Louise's advice is to start by selecting the herbs and spices you like from the following basic list: parsley, rosemary, cayenne, sage, oregano, garlic powder, paprika, chives, chervil, marjoram, thyme, savory, and turmeric. Blend these together; then add lemon juice powder, ground celery seed, and ground kelp, to taste. Experiment until you find just the right proportions for your taste buds — and always, always write down what you did, so you can repeat it! Then, says Louise, you're on your way to improving the healthfulness of your diet by reducing sugar, fat, and salt.

Seafood Seasoning

While guest "cheffing" at a local restaurant, Louise Downey used this blend to make a stuffing that she spread on flounder fillets, rolled, and baked. "I ended up with a true gourmet treat," she adds.

YIELD: ABOUT 1 CUP

- ¼ cup dried chives
- ¼ cup dried sage, chopped or rubbed
- 2 tablespoons dried thyme
- 2 tablespoons dried marjoram
- 2 tablespoons parsley flakes
- 1 tablespoon ground tumeric
- 1 tablespoon ground celery seed
- 1 teaspoon coarsely ground black pepper
- 1 teaspoon garlic powder
- 1 teaspoon onion powder
- 1 teaspoon lemon juice powder
- ½ teaspoon kelp flakes

Combine all herbs and spices thoroughly. Store in an airtight container away from heat and light.

Variation. Enrich the nutritional value by adding any wild-crafted greens such as dandelion, plantain, chickweed, or nettle.

Suggested Uses

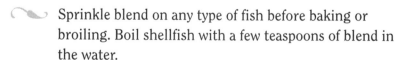

- Sprinkle blend on any type of fish before baking or broiling. Boil shellfish with a few teaspoons of blend in the water.
- Combine blend with dry bread crumbs for a coating mix that can be used on fish prior to frying or sautéing.
- For stuffing, combine blend with fresh bread crumbs and butter (1 or 2 teaspoons, to taste).

Herb Blend for Wild Game

*This very strongly flavored blend from **Broadacres Herbs** should be used sparingly. "Start with just a teaspoon in your recipe," advises co-owner Theresa Briere, "and adjust for your own taste. We eat a lot of wild game in Maine, and this recipe works well with all methods of preparation. I find it too strong for most fowl and fish, although I have used it on wild goose with great success. This recipe can also be made with fresh, finely chopped herbs."*

Broadacres Herbs
South China, Maine

Broadacres Herbs sells a variety of culinary and nonedible herb blends through their wholesale and mail-order business. The culinary blends are designed to use organically grown and wild-crafted herbs for foods such as wild game.

YIELD: APPROXIMATELY ½ CUP

    1 tablespoon dried parsley
    1 tablespoon dried marjoram
    1 tablespoon dried lemon balm
    1 tablespoon dried rosemary
    1 tablespoon dried summer savory
    2 teaspoons dried juniper berries, crushed
    1 teaspoon dried minced garlic
    1 teaspoon dried thyme
    1 teaspoon dried sage
    1 teaspoon dried mint

Combine all the herbs in an airtight jar and store away from heat and light.

Variation. Lemongrass, lemon verbena, or lemon basil are good additions. The juniper berries really add a pleasing flavor to game, so try to include them.

Suggested Uses

 Use in gravies, sauces, stuffings, or marinade.
Sprinkle on venison, moose, bear, rabbit, hare, squirrel, porcupine, woodchuck, or on beef, pork, goose, or duck.

The Herb Market
Washington, Kentucky

The Herb Market, located in a historic restoration area of Washington, Kentucky, specializes in growing scented geraniums. Owner Mary Peddie has published *The Scented Geranium Guide* and built a database of scented-geranium growers. In business since 1971, Mary was involved in the organization of the International Herb Growers and Marketers Association, as well as the Kentucky branch of this organization.

Meister Mix

*Mary Peddie of **The Herb Market** says, "Like many good recipes, the Meister Mix was an accident! Our supplier ground our mulling mix too finely, and we discovered some new uses for these spices."*

Yield: ⅞ cup

½ cup ground cinnamon
¼ cup finely ground nutmeg
2 tablespoons ground allspice

Mix spices well. Stored in an airtight container in refrigerator or freezer, blend will keep several years.

Suggested Uses

 For venison and wild game: Use 1 part salt to 3 parts Meister Mix. Rub this well into roast or steak. As marinade, use 2 tablespoons Meister Mix with 2 cups liquid (wine, vinegar, juice, or water).

 For sauerbrauten: Put 1 tablespoon sugar, 1 teaspoon salt, 2 tablespoons Meister Mix, 2 bay leaves, 1 large sliced onion, 4 cloves, 2 cups red wine, and ¼ cup vinegar and (if meat is lean) ¼ cup olive oil into a stainless steel or glass container (do not use plastic or aluminum). Marinate meat in this mixture for 24 hours or longer, turning two or three times.

MAKE IT SPICY!

 alf the challenge of cooking ethnic dishes at home is getting the spices right. The recipes in this chapter put the flavors of Mexico, India, Jamaica, and more right at your fingertips — each in one little bottle!

Many of the spices available at the grocery store are actually spice blends, such as chili powder and curry powder. By mixing these blends yourself, you'll get fresher, more pungent flavor. You may have to search a bit for some of the ingredients, although ethnic food sections in gourmet markets, health food stores, and even supermarkets are becoming more common.

These recipes give you a chance to experience lots of different types of spiciness, from the "warm" tropical spices like allspice, nutmeg, and cinnamon combined with hot peppers and ginger to the sweet spicy curry flavors of coriander, turmeric, cumin, and cayenne, and the sharp Mexican combinations of chiles, cayenne, oregano, and garlic.

Any of these spicy blends for meat can easily be converted to vegetarian use by substituting texturized vegetable protein or crumbled tofu for meat. The strong spices work especially well at giving tofu character and taste.

Devonshire Apothecary
Austin, Texas

Owner Nancy Levy says that Devonshire Apothecary's chili powder recipe is "everybody's favorite." Moreover, she notes, Texans are pretty picky about their chilis, so the popularity of this mix is a tribute to its quality. The secret is chile pequines, which are difficult to find. Nancy says they haven't found a commercial source, so they're continually searching for people who grow them. For a while they were buying them from old Mexican ladies in East Austin, but the search is ongoing. Once, Nancy notes, they came to a quick halt along a highway where someone spotted a patch of chile pequines growing.

Taos Lightning Chili Powder

*This chili powder recipe from **Devonshire Apothecary** has been used by a local Texas chef in his entry for a chili cook-off.*

YIELD: ABOUT ½ CUP

16	dried chile pequines, whole*
3	tablespoons chili powder (commercial, dark, salt-free)
4	teaspoons cayenne powder
4	teaspoons paprika
1½	teaspoons garlic granules
1½	teaspoons onion granules
1	teaspoon dried Greek oregano
1	teaspoon dried rosemary leaves, whole
1	teaspoon black peppercorns, whole
1	teaspoon cumin seeds, whole
½	teaspoon dried Mexican oregano
½	teaspoon juniper berries, whole
½	teaspoon ground ginger
½	teaspoon coriander seeds, whole
¼	teaspoon dried epazote leaf

*If you can't find pequines (the hottest around), substitute dried cayennes or chile peppers and use ½ the amount.

Mix all ingredients together and grind to a powder, or leave unground and powder it as you need it, using a small spice grinder. (We even leave it on the table with the other condiments.)

Suggested Uses

 Add this spice blend to mashed avocados (with or without chopped tomatoes) for a tangy guacamole.

 Add to beef or chicken for making tacos.

Taco Seasoning Mix

YIELD: ABOUT ⅔ CUP

¼	cup dried onion flakes
4	teaspoons cornstarch
4	tablespoons chili powder
3	teaspoons ground cumin
3	teaspoons dried garlic flakes
2	teaspoons dried hot pepper flakes
2	teaspoons beef bouillon powder
1½	teaspoons dried oregano
2	tablespoons salt (optional)

Combine all ingredients. Shake well, or place in blender for a finer blend.

Suggested Use

For beef tacos, add 3 tablespoons of this mix and ¼ cup water to 1 pound browned hamburger. Cook for 15 minutes, adding more water if needed.

Hilltop Herbery
Cazenovia, New York

Located on fifteen acres in central New York State, Mary Reeve's Hilltop Herbery sells herb plants, dried flowers, and herb-related products. She started the business nearly ten years ago, when she added a greenhouse to her property. Mary recommends growing your own herbs, because this gives you a great deal of flexibility to experiment with various blend combinations. When blending, Mary says, "Go slowly, use moderate amounts, and write it all down. Otherwise, you'll never be able to duplicate your final blend."

Mexican Gift Bag

Line a bright-color paper gift bag with another bright color of tissue paper and fill with a bag of beans, a bag of rice, and a bottle of Taos Lightning Chili Powder or Taco Seasoning Mix. Add a bottle of specialty hot sauce and give it to one of your spicy-food-loving friends!

Thyme & Seasons Books
Bertram, Texas

Susan Wittig Albert, a former college English professor, has found a rather unusual way to combine her love of herbs with her passion for writing — writing herbal mysteries. Her China Bayles Mystery Series (published in hardcover by Charles Scribner's Sons and in paperback by Berkley Mystery) has been widely acclaimed. The first book, *Thyme of Death,* was published in 1992; as of 1996 Susan has produced three more titles in the series: *Witches' Bane, Hangman's Root,* and *Rosemary Remembered.* She and her husband, Bill, sell these titles, along with small-press and self-published books, through their company, Thyme & Seasons Books. They also publish a seasonal newsletter entitled *China's Garden.*

Mexican Marinade Mix

*Susan Wittig Albert, of **Thyme & Seasons Books** and author of the China Bayles Mystery series, enjoys sharing these south-of-the-border flavors because all her books are set in Texas.*

YIELD: ABOUT ⅓ CUP

  ½ teaspoon salt
  2½ teaspoons dried oregano
  2½ teaspoons dried cumin
  2½ teaspoons ground chile pepper
  2½ teaspoons ground cloves
  2½ teaspoons ground cinnamon
  2½ teaspoons ground black pepper
  1 teaspoon garlic powder

Blend ingredients thoroughly.

Suggested Use

 To make marinade, combine 3 teaspoons mix with ½ cup chopped onion, 1 tablespoon olive oil, and 1 cup red-wine vinegar. This is enough to marinate 1 pound of beef. Also good for marinating kabobs and grilled steak.

Chorizo Seasoning (Mexican Pork Sausage)

*Another spicy blend from **Thyme & Seasons Books**.*

YIELD: ABOUT ½ CUP (ENOUGH TO SEASON 2½ POUNDS
LEAN PORK SAUSAGE)

- ¼ cup ground chile pepper, mild or hot depending on taste
- 2 teaspoons garlic powder
- 2 teaspoons onion
- 1½ teaspoons ground cumin
- 1 teaspoon dried oregano
- 1 teaspoon ground cinnamon
- 1 teaspoon salt

Blend all ingredients thoroughly.

Suggested Use

 Combine ½ cup cider vinegar and (if preferred) ¼ cup Tequila with ½ cup seasoning mixture and add to 2½ pounds lean pork sausage. Olé!

Choosing Chiles

Chili powder (as opposed to a chile pepper) is usually a mixture of dried chiles, garlic, oregano, cumin, coriander, and cloves. Where a recipe calls for chile peppers you can use any kind of pepper that you happen to have or to like. If you are a gardener, you'll find dozens of different kinds of peppers available in seed catalogs.

Herbs-Liscious
Marshalltown, Iowa

Carol Lacko-Beem enjoys "spreading the herb word" and acting as a resource on obscure herbal knowledge for individuals and organizations. She operates Herbs-Liscious out of her home in a suburban neighborhood in central Iowa. Carol grows her herbs in the yard and in a small greenhouse, and sells a complete line of herbs, herbal products, and herb-related items through a mail-order catalog.

Herb Chili-Liscious Mix

*Carol Lacko-Beem of **Herbs-Liscious** developed this easy-to-make chili blend — good to have on hand for cooking up a pot of chili anytime.*

YIELD: ABOUT ½ CUP

3	tablespoons chili powder blend
1½	tablespoons onion granules
2	teaspoons garlic granules
1½	teaspoons dried oregano
1	teaspoon dried lovage, or ⅛ teaspoon ground celery
1	teaspoon dried marjoram
¾	teaspoon dried thyme
½	teaspoon paprika
¼	teaspoon ground cumin
¼	teaspoon cayenne powder
⅛	teaspoon ground coriander
¼	teaspoon ground ginger
⅛	teaspoon ground allspice
⅛	teaspoon ground cloves

Mix together all herbs and spices. Store in an airtight container. For a milder blend, decrease the amounts of chili powder and cayenne.

Suggested Use

 To make chili: add ½ cup mix and 2–3 bay leaves to 1 pound extra lean ground beef, 6–8 cups cooked beans, and 1 quart tomatoes. During 10 minutes of cooking, add one small red chile pepper. The longer you leave chile pepper in chili, the hotter it will become, so take care. Remove chile pepper and bay leaves before serving.

Spicy Jamaican Blend

*Maribeth Johnson of **Mari-Mann Herb Company** has found that people who have visited Jamaica are particularly enthusiastic about this rub for meat and fish. Moreover, Maribeth notes, food scientists are discovering that hot sauces not only destroy food bacteria, but have many health benefits.*

YIELD: ABOUT ½ CUP

>   6 tablespoons ground allspice
>   3 teaspoons ground black pepper
> 1½ teaspoons ground nutmeg
> 1½ teaspoons ground cinnamon
> 1½ teaspoons salt (optional)

Mix spices thoroughly.

Variation. Lemon zest (½ teaspoon) adds a nice flavor.

Suggested Use

 To make rub, combine 2¾ tablespoons of the Spicy Jamaican Blend with 1 jalapeño pepper, cored, seeded and chopped, 1 tablespoon freshly grated ginger, 2 cloves garlic (crushed), and 2 tablespoons vegetable oil. Mix all ingredients well, and rub onto fish, beef, lamb, or pork. Grill until done. Jalapeño pepper may be increased or decreased according to taste.

Mari-Mann Herb Co., Inc.
Decatur, Illinois

Maribeth Johnson's main interest is educating the public about the many aspects of using herbs, spices, and everlasting dried flowers. She began selling herbs out of her home in 1976 and in 1978 expanded to a twelve-acre farm housing gardens, a gift shop, tearoom, and lots of room for teaching. Mari-Mann's educational activities include cooking, craft, and gardening classes, and their teaching staff boasts noted chefs, including the chairman of the board of Central Illinois Chefs. Their annual not-for-profit Herb Fest held on Mother's Day weekend gathers together herb specialists from around the world to share their knowledge and skills with the public.

Bittersweet Herb Farm
Charlemont, Massachusetts

Located on the historic Mohawk Trail in western Massachusetts, Bittersweet Herb Farm is primarily a wholesale business although they plan to open a retail outlet in spring 1996. They specialize in packaging herb and spice blends for the gift market, which they show at craft and flower shows along the Eastern seaboard. Jill Wallace is particularly proud of the prize ribbons they have won for best booth design at the Philadelphia Flower Show several years running.

Cajun Herb Mix

*Jill Wallace of **Bittersweet Herb Farm** developed this spicy seasoning for meat, poultry, and fish after discovering the joys of Cajun food.*

YIELD: ⅔ CUP

5	tablespoons paprika
2	tablespoons granulated garlic
2	tablespoons dried onion flakes
1½	teaspoons dried oregano
1½	teaspoons dried basil
1	tablespoon cayenne powder
1½	teaspoons ground white pepper

Mix all ingredients together. For a milder blend, decrease the amount of cayenne by ½.

Variation. Salt may be added to herb mix or after meat is cooked, if needed.

Suggested Uses

 For grilling, dredge chicken, fish (swordfish, tuna, or salmon), or steak through the mix before placing it on the grill.

 This mix also makes a spicy dip or sauce. Add to sour cream, mayonnaise, or yogurt and serve with chips or cut-up vegetables.

Fanny Couch's Mild Curry Powder

*This easy, mild blend from **Thyme & Seasons Books** is built out of the "basic four" curry spices: coriander, turmeric, cumin, and fenugreek, with the addition of cloves and cardamom and a hint of cayenne. Since coriander dominates in this blend, the taste is sweet and the aroma is fruity, with an anise overtone.*

YIELD: ABOUT ¾ CUP

    6 tablespoons dried coriander
1½ tablespoons ground turmeric
1½ tablespoons ground cumin
1½ tablespoons ground fenugreek
1½ teaspoons ground cloves
1½ teaspoons ground cardamom
 ⅛ teaspoon cayenne powder

Blend and store in a tightly capped jar away from heat and light.

Suggested Use

This mild curry can be used with delicately flavored dishes such as fish or vegetables, and even fruit.

Thyme & Seasons Books
Bertram, Texas

Mystery writer and herbalist Susan Wittig Albert has a lot of fun melding her two careers. One way she does this is to feature columns in her newsletter "China's Garden" with the bylines of characters from her China Bayles mystery novels. The curry recipes featured on this and the following pages come from "seventy-something Fanny Couch, the 'Talkshow Lady' of Pecan Springs," the fictional town in which Susan's novels are set. Fanny hosts a weekday morning radio show called "Fanny's Back Fence," which welcomes calls from listeners who want to share their stories, gripes, opinions, and recipes. These are the recipes from Fanny's show focusing on curries.

Devilishly Good Curried Eggs

4 hard-boiled eggs
½ cup minced onion
2 teaspoons minced red sweet pepper
1 teaspoon mild or pungent curry powder
½ teaspoon salt
¼ teaspoon dry mustard
⅛ teaspoon sugar
⅛ teaspoon chili powder blend
1 teaspoon lemon juice

Slice boiled eggs lengthwise, remove yolks. Mash and mix with all ingredients. Refill whites, garnish with bits of red pepper and parsley.

Fanny Couch's Pungent Curry Powder

*This spice blend from **Thyme & Seasons Books** uses the "basic four," with coriander predominant, along with equal amounts of black pepper, poppy seed, ginger, ground red chile, as well as mustard and cardamom.*

YIELD: ABOUT ⅔ CUP

4 tablespoons dried coriander
2 tablespoons ground turmeric
1½ tablespoons ground cumin
1 tablespoon ground fenugreek
1½ teaspoons ground black pepper
1½ teaspoons poppy seeds
1½ teaspoons ground ginger
1½ teaspoons ground, dried red chile
¾ teaspoon dried mustard
½ teaspoon ground cardamom

Blend and store in a tightly capped jar away from heat and light.

Suggested Use

 Use this powerful curry to flavor meat dishes, either as a condiment or in the sauce.

Coralee's Chic Chicken Curry

As Thyme & Season Books' Fanny Couch tells it, "A couple of years ago, Coralee Tarp won the annual Myra Merryweather Herb Cook-Off with this elegant curry. The prize was a concrete chicken crafted by Homer Thompson, which everybody thought was wonderfully appropriate. Unfortunately, Coralee dropped her chicken in the parking lot and broke it to smithereens. Luckily, Homer had another one in the trunk of his car, so Coralee got her concrete chicken after all."

    4   tablespoons olive oil
    2   onions, chopped
    4   tablespoons mild or pungent curry powder
    1   cup chicken broth
    4   cups cooked chicken, cubed
    2   cups pineapple chunks
    2   bananas, sliced
    1   green apple, chopped
    1   cup shredded coconut
    ½   cup chopped almonds
    ½   cup mango chutney
    1   cucumber, chopped
    1   tablespoon lemon juice
    1   cup half-and-half

Prepare all sliced and chopped ingredients. Sauté onion in oil for 6–7 minutes, add curry powder and cook for 2–3 minutes, then add broth. Add everything else but the half and half, reduce heat, and cook covered for 2 minutes, until the fruit is just tender. Stir in half-and-half just before serving.

Curried Apricot Cookies

Fanny says, "Leila Long made up this recipe by mistake. She thought she'd got the cinnamon, but it turned out to be curry. A delicious mistake!"

    1   cup margarine
    2   cups brown sugar
    1   teaspoon vanilla
    2   eggs
    ¾   cup chopped walnuts
    ¾   cup diced dried
        apricots
    3   cups unbleached flour
    ½   teaspoon baking soda
    1   teaspoon baking
        powder
    2   teaspoons mild or
        pungent curry powder

Preheat oven to 325°F. Cream margarine and sugar, add vanilla, eggs. Blend all other ingredients and add to the creamed mixture. Chill until stiff. Roll into balls, place on nonstick cookie sheet, and flatten with a fork. Bake until golden.

CHAPTER 6

Italian Seasonings

A bottle of Italian seasoning blend is probably one of the most popular and most used bottles in the average spice rack. The recipes in this chapter show how many different ways there are to combine the classic Italian herbs — basil, parsley, thyme, and oregano.

The popularity of pasta as a health food in recent years has broadened the definition of Italian food. The general image is pasta served with tomato sauce, but there are so many other ways to make sauce — especially with an herb blend. A little bit of cream or (for a lower-fat version) evaporated skimmed milk combined with one of these Italian seasoning blends and Parmesan cheese makes a great, yet simple, pasta sauce. Add some sautéed vegetables for extra flavor.

The pesto recipes in this chapter offer many more variations on pasta. Other than in the classic basil pesto which relies mainly on basil, you can use a base of parsley and pine nuts in oil and then add other herbs to taste. The lemon herbs such as sorrel lemon, lemon thyme, and lemon basil make flavorful pestos. There are many different flavors of basil, as well. Let your imagination run wild. How about fresh berry pasta (which is raspberry flavored) with a cinnamon basil pesto served as a dessert pasta?

Good Thyme Farm
Bethlehem, Connecticut

Eileen Mendyka began her business in scenic Litchfield County to meet the needs of area chefs who were asking for good fresh herbs. "They convinced me to start and they were my first customers," says Eileen. Her small, family-operated business continues to specialize in culinary herbs and edible flowers.

For home growers of herbs, Eileen recommends learning each herb's growing habits and using it in season when it's at its peak flavor. She also encourages trying special varieties of herbs, such as Genovese and lemon basils. When you know the individual herbs well, you will be successful at combining them in blends, Eileen notes.

Basil Pesto

*Eileen Mendyka of **Good Thyme Farm** says this blend is "great on almost everything!"*

YIELD: ABOUT 2 CUPS

> 4 cups fresh basil leaves
> 4–6 cloves garlic
> ¾ cup toasted pignoli nuts
> ½ cup fresh parsley leaves
> 1 teaspoon salt (optional)
> 1 cup olive oil
> ¾ cup freshly grated Parmesan

Place all ingredients except olive oil and cheese in food processor. Slowly add oil and process to a chunky paste (do not overprocess). Add more oil if needed. Fold in cheese. Store up to one week in the refrigerator or for several months in the freezer in an airtight container.

Suggested Uses

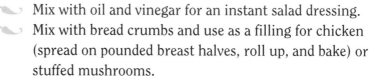

Spread on tomato halves and broil.

Mix with oil and vinegar for an instant salad dressing.

Mix with bread crumbs and use as a filling for chicken (spread on pounded breast halves, roll up, and bake) or stuffed mushrooms.

Serve over pasta.

Rosemary—Black Olive Pesto

*This pesto variation from **Good Thyme Farm** proves you can have pesto even when you don't have basil.*

YIELD: ABOUT 2½ CUPS

- ⅓ cup fresh rosemary leaves
- 1 cup fresh parsley leaves
- 2–3 cloves garlic
- ½ cup walnuts
- ½ cup pitted black olives
- ½ cup olive oil
- ½ cup freshly grated Parmesan

Place all ingredients except olive oil and cheese in food processor. Slowly add oil and process to a chunky paste (do not overprocess). Add more oil if needed. Fold in cheese. Store up to one week in the refrigerator or several months in the freezer in an airtight container.

Suggested Use

 Excellent with lamb, either spread on cooked meat or mixed with drippings for a great sauce. Also goes well with other red meats and mushrooms.

Sorrel-Lemon Pesto

*Yet another pesto variation from **Good Thyme Farm.***

Yield: About 1 cup

    2 cups fresh sorrel (remove center vein)
    ¾ cup fresh basil leaves
    ½ cup fresh parsley leaves
 2–3 cloves garlic
    1 teaspoon fresh lemon juice
    ½ cup toasted pignoli nuts
    ½ teaspoon salt (optional)
    ¼ cup olive oil

Place all dry ingredients in food processor. Slowly add oil and process to a chunky paste (do not overprocess). Add more oil if needed. Store up to one week in the refrigerator or several months in the freezer.

Suggested Uses

 Excellent on fish (spread on broiled fish such as salmon just before serving).
 Great on cold seafood/pasta salad, or on cold shrimp or scallop appetizers.

Herb Seasoning for Pasta

This classic blend of Italian seasonings comes from Kathleen Gips' Village Herb Shop.

YIELD: APPROXIMATELY ⅔ CUP

    3 tablespoons dried basil
    3 tablespoons dried parsley
    3 tablespoons dried oregano
    1 tablespoon garlic granules

Combine all ingredients and store in airtight container. When adding to foods, crush herbs with fingers.

Suggested Use

Mix 1 cup herb blend with ¼ cup melted butter or olive oil. Toss with warm pasta. Allow ½ teaspoon per serving.

Kathleen Gips' Village Herb Shop/Pine Creek Herbs
Chagrin Falls, Ohio

Kathleen Gips creates an extensive "herbal pantry" of products for her customers, including herb jellies, vinegars, herb and flower teas, and herb seasoning mixes. She recommends using only organically grown herbs and drying them in a warm, dry, dimly lit spot. Leaves dry faster when stripped from the stem, Kathleen notes. She suggests placing the leaves on top of the refrigerator for fast drying.

Flavor Your Own Pesto

You can make any flavor of pesto by using parsley as a base and adding small amounts of your favorite herbs, along with garlic, oil, cheese, and nuts. Try experimenting with adding small amounts of nut-flavored olive oils, as well, such as walnut, almond, and even macadamia nut.

Sunrise Herb Farm
Bethel, Connecticut

Owner Valerie Hawk began her venture into the world of cooking with herbs at age sixteen when she launched a catering business. She had some good guidance from her aunt Sheila Lukins, co-author of *The Silver Palate* cookbooks. Valerie continued her pursuit of herb cookery with a degree in business and culinary arts, and graduate study in the culinary, medicinal, cosmetic, and craft uses of herbs.

Valerie shares her love of herbs with the public at Sunrise Herb Farm, offering an array of herb plants from around the world, herbal cosmetics, natural gifts, and herbal soups, breads, cakes, and teas, which are served throughout the day. One of her specialties is herbal- and floral-flavored ice creams. The farm also houses an herb and garden library and offers a wide variety of weekend classes.

Lemon Balm–Spearmint Pesto

Valerie Hawk of **Sunrise Herb Farm** *developed this light pesto variation.*

YIELD: ABOUT 1 CUP

   2 cups fresh lemon balm and spearmint leaves
½ cup olive oil
½ cup garlic cloves

Chop and blend all ingredients together. This blend can be stored frozen for two to three months in an airtight container.

Suggested Use

   Ideal pesto to use as a fresh summer sauce on fish.

Finding Flavorful Oregano

Oregano is a very important part of an Italian blend, and it comes in many different flavors. A lot of the oregano that you find in the store has no flavor. Right now, the oregano that most consistently has good flavor is labeled "Greek oregano," which is why some of the recipes include that designation. If you're buying oregano fresh or in bulk dried, scratch and sniff it before buying.

Food Emporium Italian Seasoning

*Nancy Tapp of **Thomson Herb Farm Food Emporium** says, "Even Santa loves our Italian seasoning. Every Christmas season our neighbor, a hog farmer, changes his overalls for a Santa suit and helps us with our Food Emporium festivities. In return, we keep him supplied with our seasoning for the year, which comes to about 2 quarts. He thinks he is the winner in this arrangement, but we know we are the lucky ones."*

YIELD: ABOUT 4 CUPS

- 1 cup dried basil
- 1 cup dried parsley
- ½ cup dried Greek oregano
- ½ cup dried minced onion
- ¼ cup dried thyme
- ½ cup dried minced garlic
- ⅛ cup crushed mild dried chile peppers, such as 'New Mexico'
- 1 tablespoon ground black pepper
- 1 tablespoon dried sage

Combine the ingredients in a large bowl and blend thoroughly. Keep in clean airtight glass jars in a cupboard or dark place to prevent fading and loss of flavor.

Suggested Uses

- For instant spaghetti sauce, mix 1 tablespoon seasoning with 1 cup tomatoes and cook for 15 minutes.
- Add seasoning to pizza sauce, meatballs, Italian hamburgers (with mozzerella cheese on top), pasta salad, steamed summer squash, garlic bread, and salad dressing.

Thomson Herb Farm Food Emporium
Holliday, Missouri

Located in the gentle rolling hills of northern Missouri, Thomson Herb Farm is a haven for herb lovers. The farm's Food Emporium includes: a country store (featuring their own spice blends, herbal vinegars, and herbal gifts); a dining room serving (by reservation only) lunch, afternoon tea, and dinner prepared with fresh herbs and vegetables from their gardens; a cooking school featuring guest chefs teaching gourmet cooking; and a guest house for those seeking a getaway in the country (but with gourmet dining!). The farm is also home to a nursery that sells potted plants and offers an herb display garden.

Richland Creek Herb Farm
Seagrove, North Carolina

Richland Creek Herb Farm advises creative cooks who want to experiment with developing their own blends to take a cup out of what you're cooking and to it add the herbs you want to try. This way, you can try several different seasonings for the same dish — and you don't end up wasting too much food if there's a blend you don't like!

Herbal Supreme Meat or Pasta Blend

This recipe for spicy meatballs was developed by Richland Creek Herb Farm.

YIELD: ABOUT 1⅓ CUPS

- ½ cup dried chives
- ¼ cup dried basil
- ¼ cup dried lovage
- 1 tablespoon dried oregano
- 1 tablespoon dried thyme
- ½ teaspoon ground nutmeg

Mix together all the ingredients and blend well.

Suggested Uses

 For meatballs: Combine ⅔ cup herb blend with 1 tablespoon freshly chopped jalapeño pepper. Add 1 pound ground beef or 1 pound ground pork. Form into meatballs and brown in frying pan. This recipe makes enough beef meatballs for 1 pound of spaghetti. We have served pork meatballs at Herbfest on toothpicks without sauce to let people taste the herbs.

 For vegetarian pasta: Cook 1 pound of spaghetti or other pasta and drain. Heat 2 tablespoons of butter and ⅔ cup Herbal Supreme Meat or Pasta Blend. Add one 16-ounce can of crushed tomatoes, one 16-ounce can tomato sauce, and ⅓ cup sugar. Serve warmed sauce over pasta.

Lambs & Thyme Spaghetti Herbs

*This spaghetti sauce seasoning recipe from **Lambs & Thyme at Randallane** could easily become a spice rack staple.*

1 teaspoon dried rosemary
½ teaspoon dried oregano
½ teaspoon fennel seeds
½ teaspoon garlic powder
¼ teaspoon ground black pepper

Mix ingredients to blend. Make up a batch or two to have ready for use in all tomato dishes for that Old World taste.

Suggested Uses

 Sprinkle herb mixture to taste into your spaghetti sauce while it simmers.
 Sprinkle herb mixture on vegetables, fish, and manicotti.

Lambs & Thyme at Randallane
Richmond, New Hampshire

The name "Lambs & Thyme" was chosen by owners David and Judith Grave to reflect that their farm is home to sheep (whose wool is used in many of the crafts made on the farm), as well as thyme (and "time," since the Graves are retired. Although, Judith notes, they really don't have much of the latter). Lambs & Thyme carries 120 products using herbs, including a broad selection of culinary blends. "Herbs turn any ordinary meal into gourmet and have so many health benefits," says Judith. She recommends introducing a few new herbs to your garden each year, and taking the time to fully study and experiment with the taste each one adds.

Herb Mix for Italian Breads

Frog Park Herbs
Waterville, New York

Owner Bonnie Dobmeier notes that she began making Italian bread blends soon after she started Frog Park Herbs in 1978, which was long before bruschetta and foccaccia became chic at American tables. Today, this is one of the popular gourmet herb blends that keeps this family enterprise thriving. Located in the foothills of the Adirondack Mountains in central New York State, Frog Park Herbs also sells plants in season and seeds, and maintains a year-round retail store featuring herb-related crafts in nearby Sherrill, New York.

*This mixture from **Frog Park Herbs** brings specialty Italian breads right to your kitchen.*

YIELD: APPROXIMATELY 1 CUP

¼ cup dried garlic granules
¼ cup dried minced garlic
¼ cup dried basil
¼ cup dried parsley
1 tablespoon paprika
1 teaspoon ground black pepper
½ teaspoon ground red pepper (optional)

Combine ingredients and mix well. Label and store in glass jar with airtight lid away from heat and light.

Suggested Uses

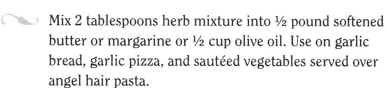

Mix 2 tablespoons herb mixture into ½ pound softened butter or margarine or ½ cup olive oil. Use on garlic bread, garlic pizza, and sautéed vegetables served over angel hair pasta.

Italian Garlic Bread: Combine 2 tablespoons herb mixture with ½ pound butter or margarine. Cut a loaf of Italian bread in half lengthwise and brush with butter/ herb mixture. Sprinkle with grated Parmesan cheese. Place on a baking sheet and broil 3 to 5 minutes until lightly browned.

Bruschetta: Combine 2 tablespoons herb mixture with ½ cup olive oil. Toast Italian bread slices. Brush with oil/ herb mixture. Top each slice with 2 tablespoons chopped vegetables (such as tomatoes, spinach, onion, fresh basil, and zucchini). Sprinkle with grated mozzarella cheese. Place slices on a baking sheet and broil 3 to 5 minutes until bubbling and browned.

Veggie Pasta: Combine 2 tablespoons herb mixture with ½ cup olive oil. Pare and slice a selection of fresh vegetables (tomatoes, zucchini, mushrooms, onions, green peppers, and spinach). Sauté vegetables in olive oil/herb mixture. Cook angel hair pasta; toss with vegetables and top with grated Romano cheese. This makes a wonderful light supper.

Red and Green Pizza Garlicky Blend

Sweet Posie Herbary says, "We are a spicy bunch and truly enjoy this blend."

YIELD: ⅓ CUP

>   2 tablespoons dried oregano
>   1 tablespoon dried basil
>   ½ tablespoon fennel seeds, crushed
>   ½ tablespoon dried thyme
>   1 teaspoon garlic granules
>   1 tablespoon cayenne pepper flakes

Combine all ingredients and store in an airtight jar away from heat and light.

Suggested Uses

 Sprinkle this blend on anything that needs a jolt: spaghetti, chili, minestrone, and so on — especially pizza!

Sweet Posie Herbary
Johnsonburg, Pennsylvania

Following many years of gardening and crafting with herbs and perennials, master gardener Stephanie Distler is one of the newcomers to the herb business world. "I wanted to do something that my whole family could be included in," says Stephanie, "and what better way than an herb business." Her shop is nestled among two period gardens, three theme gardens, and a vegetable and everlasting garden. Her shop stocks herb and spice blends, vinegars, bouquet garni bags, jellies, teas, and an array of herbal crafts and beauty-care products.

Thorp's Igloo Grown Herbs
Atlantic, Pennsylvania

Thorp's Igloo Grown Herbs takes its unusual name from the fact that both their home and greenhouse are located in former TNT concrete bunkers. These storage facilities are among 100 designed and built by the U.S. government to house explosives produced at the Kestone TNT factory. While the bunkers were never actually used for that purpose, they have been reclaimed by farmers and families to use as homes and barns.

The Thorp family enterprise is dedicated to producing organically grown herbs, heirloom vegetables, and plants. They currently offer over three hundred varieties, as well as a selection of gourmet whole-leaf dried culinary and tea blends made on the premises.

Thorpe's Igloo Italian Blend

*This blend from **Thorp's Igloo Grown Herbs** makes a good base flavor for many dishes. The ingredients can be grown by anyone with a small herb garden. To retain the best flavor, the Thorps suggest keeping herbs as whole as possible and only crushing as much of this mix as you can use in two months.*

YIELD: ½ CUP

- 3 tablespoons dried Greek oregano
- 2 tablespoons dried Italian (flat-leaf) parsley
- 2 tablespoons dried purple or green basil
- 1 tablespoon dried bronze or green fennel leaves

Combine all ingredients and crush to blend.

Suggested Uses

 Use on pizza, breads, butters, dips made with sour cream or cheese, and vinegars.

Add blend to tomato sauce, just for last 15 minutes of cooking for best flavor. To cut the acid flavor of fresh tomatoes, try adding hot peppers, Welsh onions, garlic, or green peppers. For sweetness, add cinnamon basil.

For pesto: Add fresh herbs to food processor and blend with enough oil to make a thick paste.

A Gift of Pasta

Everybody loves an Italian gift package. Buy an inexpensive pasta bowl and fill it with some Italian seasoning blends, fun-shaped pasta, a jar of home-canned tomatoes, and a pound of fresh mozzarella. A bottle of extra virgin olive oil is always a treat. This makes a great housewarming gift.

SPECIALTY BLENDS

This chapter includes traditional blends from various cuisines including French, Thai, and Moroccan, as well as some blends especially for particular foods such as beans, rice and other grains, or soups.

There are a great variety of taste sensations in this chapter. The Melrose Mix is a great one. The Herbes de Provence could be used on roast pork as well as lamb and seafood, and would make a good marinade with some vinegar and olive oil for grilled pork.

The Thai blend has mint and lemon zest. For Americans, this flavor combination of the hot and the sweet and the sour is unusual, but it really makes these foods interesting. If you don't have access to the lemongrass, you can use lemon verbena.

The Moroccan blend also utilizes mint, if you're a gardener with mint in your yard. It's interesting cuisine because it has influences from a lot of different areas, including northern Africa and India. This blend makes a great marinade for lamb as well as pork, chicken, or grilled tofu. The rice and soup blends are good starting points for making many basic dishes. Finally, the zucchini blend will be appreciated by any gardener who is in search of new ways to use zucchini.

Elderflower Farm
Roseburg, Oregon

Located on a mountainside about sixty miles from the Oregon coast, Elderflower Farm finds the temperate climate ideal for growing herbs. "It's really a Mediterranean climate," note owners John and Kelly Stelzer.

John and Kelly have been making herb blends commercially for about seventeen years from the sixty varieties of organic herbs they grow, combined with spices they buy from the purest sources available. "Although we have grown to a point where we have to buy herbs from other sources to reach our annual production goals," notes Kelly, "we always use organic Oregon-grown herbs, and we still do everything by hand. We haven't compromised our quality; in fact, we try to make it better every year."

Herbes de Provence

*This is the newest herb blend from **Elderflower Farm**. Several of their local customers requested it because of their nostalgia for the regional specialties in France they remembered. Traditionally made from a combination of fennel, lavender, marjoram, rosemary, savory, and thyme, Herbes de Provence may also contain bay and sage.*

YIELD: ¾ CUP

    4 tablespoons dried thyme
    2 tablespoons dried marjoram
    1 tablespoon dried rosemary
    1 tablespoon dried savory
    2 teaspoons dried lavender flowers
    1 teaspoon fennel seeds

Mix ingredients to blend.

Suggested Use

 This is excellent in tomato dishes such as bouillabaisse, and with lamb.

Scallops Provençal

YIELD: 4 SERVINGS

    2 shallots, minced
    1 small clove garlic, minced
    2 teaspoons olive oil
    8 large peeled Italian tomatoes, coarsely chopped
    1 teaspoon Herbes de Provence
    1 pound fresh scallops
    2 tablespoons fresh parsley, minced

Sauté the shallots and garlic quickly in the olive oil, stirring constantly to prevent browning. Add the tomatoes when the shallots are translucent. Stir, add the Herbes de Provence, and simmer 10 minutes to blend flavors and cook off some of the liquid. Stir in the scallops and cook until just done — 3 to 5 minutes. Remove from heat. Stir in parsley and serve immediately.

Thai Blend

Elderflower Farm developed this recipe to give as a gift to a friend who had been to Thailand and raved about the food.

YIELD: ABOUT ½ CUP

    4 tablespoons dried mint
    2 tablespoons dried lemon zest
    4 teaspoons ground white pepper
    2 teaspoons ground black pepper
    2 teaspoons dried lemongrass
    ¼ teaspoon ground cumin
    ½ teaspoon cayenne powder

Mix ingredients and grind finely in a spice grinder or blender.

Variation. If you can't find lemongrass, use lemon verbena leaves.

Thai Roll-Ups

A Thai appetizer.

YIELD: 12 ROLL-UPS

½ pound ground chicken
3 garlic cloves, minced
4–6 tablespoons chicken broth or stock
2 tablespoons green onions, finely chopped
1 tablespoon fresh cilantro, finely chopped
1 tablespoon Thai Blend
3 tablespoons lime juice
1 tablespoon Nam Pla (fish sauce)
12 lettuce leaves, washed and drained

Heat 2 tablespoons broth to boiling in a sauté pan, add chicken and garlic, and stir fry. Continue adding broth as needed until chicken is cooked. Remove from heat and thoroughly mix in onions, herbs, lime juice, and Nam Pla. Spoon the mixture onto lettuce leaves, wrap up sides, and eat with the fingers.

Melrose Mix

This is another of the fourteen specialty blends John and Kelly Stelzer of Elderflower Farm make from organically grown herbs.

YIELD: ABOUT ½ CUP

    3 tablespoons dried oregano
    2 tablespoons dried sage
    1 tablespoon dried savory
    1 tablespoon dried horseradish leaves
    ½ tablespoon dried heal-all flowers
    1 teaspoon dried chive flowers
    ½ teaspoon dried Russian tarragon
    ½ teaspoon dried opal basil
    ½ teaspoon dried lavender

Mix ingredients to blend and store in airtight container away from heat and light.

Suggested Uses

 Excellent in rice dishes, long-cooking dishes such as soups and stews, and in casseroles.

Lamb Stew

YIELD: 4 SERVINGS

½ cup flour
  Salt and pepper to taste
1 pound lamb stew meat
2 tablespoons olive oil
1 clove garlic
4 or 5 shallots
½ pound mushrooms
1 pint tomatoes
½ cup black olives, sliced
¼ cup currants
1 teaspoon Melrose Mix
1 teaspoon paprika
½ cup fresh parsley
2 pounds small red potatoes, scrubbed and boiled

Put the flour, salt, and pepper in a bag, and add the lamb. Shake lightly to coat the meat. Heat the olive oil in a skillet. Brown the garlic slowly to flavor the oil and then remove garlic. Add lamb, and brown. Add the shallots and mushrooms. Sauté until browned.

Add the tomatoes into the pan, and bring to a boil. Lower the heat, add the olives and currants, and simmer until the lamb is cooked through and tender. Stir in the Melrose Mix and paprika; heat. Stir in the parsley, and serve stew with whole boiled red potatoes.

Simpson's Country Herb Farm
Jefferson, Oregon

The herb and tea shop of Simpson's Country Herb Farm is housed in the original kitchen of an 1880s Victorian-style farmhouse ten miles south of Salem, Oregon. Owner Kathleen Simpson notes that the original built-in cabinets are still present — filled now with herbs, spices, and tea blends. The house's other claim to fame is that Clark Gable lived and worked there as a handyman before going to Hollywood. Even after being discovered, Gable returned to the house for a short time to learn to ride a horse for an upcoming movie.

The farm's nine acres are also home to an herb nursery and gardens. The Simpsons sell a large variety of fresh herb plants from the greenhouse and over two hundred dried herbs and spices through their mail-order catalog.

Moroccan Spice Blend

Kathleen Simpson of Simpson's Country Herb Farm created this recipe for her husband David's favorite meal, shish kebab with pilaf. For superior flavor, Kathleen recommends using whole spices and grinding them yourself with a coffee or spice grinder before blending.

YIELD: ABOUT 4½ CUPS

1½	cups dried cilantro
1½	cups dried parsley
1	cup dried mint
3	tablespoons dried onion flakes
2	tablespoons dried marjoram
1	tablespoon ground cumin
1	teaspoon ground cinnamon
1	teaspoon white pepper
¾	teaspoon cayenne powder
¼	teaspoon ground cloves
¼	teaspoon ground cardamom seeds
¼	teaspoon ground nutmeg

Combine ingredients, mixing well. Store in airtight container in a cool, dark place.

Suggested Uses

 This is an excellent seasoning for lamb and is also good on vegetables. Use it to season casseroles or pilaf.

 Make a marinade for lamb dishes such as shish kebabs by combining ¼ cup Moroccan Spice Blend with 1 cup dry red wine and ½ cup olive oil.

Rose Manor Rice Seasoning

With this recipe from Rose Manor Bed & Breakfast, you won't need to spend any more money on expensive boxed mixes.

YIELD: ABOUT ½ CUP

   2 tablespoons dried parsley
   2 tablespoons dried basil
   2 tablespoons instant chicken bouillon granules
   2 teaspoons onion powder
   ¾ teaspoon garlic powder
   ¼ teaspoon dried thyme

Combine ingredients in a glass container with a tight-fitting lid.

Seasoned Rice Pilaf

YIELD: ABOUT 3½ CUPS

   3½ tablespoons Rose Manor Rice Seasoning
   1½ cups uncooked long grain rice
   10 pieces spaghetti, broken into ½" pieces
   2½ cups water
    1 tablespoon butter

Combine Rose Manor Rice Seasoning with rice and spaghetti pieces. Add water and butter, stir. Bring to a boil. Reduce heat, cover, and simmer 15 to 20 minutes, stirring occasionally to prevent sticking.

Rose Manor Bed & Breakfast
Manheim, Pennsylvania

Owner Susan Jenal began her business selling herbs out of an apartment in downtown Manhattan, under the name Lady Slipper Herbal Creations. In 1995, she purchased Rose Manor, a bed & breakfast inn in Lancaster County, Pennsylvania. Her interest in herbs is reflected in the cooking and decor of the inn. In addition, the inn houses an herb-related gift shop and is surrounded by herb and rose gardens. Susan also sells herbal products through a wholesale catalog. The inn serves afternoon tea by appointment, as well as hosting overnight guests.

Arie's Herb Gardens
Sylacauga, Alabama

Partners Wanda Rayfield and Penny Moore are both schoolteachers. Their interest in herbs goes back to 1989, when Wanda's eighth-grade English class read *Foxfire*. The students became interested in Aunt Arie, the herb lady of the Appalachian Mountains. As a class project, they planted herb seeds in milk cartons and grew them on the classroom windowsills. When Wanda was left with six plants at the end of the school year, she took them home to plant. As the plants flourished, Wanda and Penny sought to identify them — thus began their "herbal education" and love of growing herbs.

Arie's Herb and Rice Mix

*This blend from **Arie's Herb Gardens** makes a terrific holiday gift. Try packaging it with Arie's Herb & Butter Mix (see page 24).*

Yield: 1 cup uncooked rice (makes about 2½ cups cooked)

    1 cup uncooked rice
    1 beef bouillon cube
    ½ teaspoon salt
    ½ teaspoon dried marjoram
    ½ teaspoon dried thyme leaves
    1 teaspoon dried scallion flakes

Mix ingredients and put in plastic bag. Keep airtight.

Suggested Use

 To cook, combine rice mixture with 2 cups cold water and 1 tablespoon butter in heavy saucepan. Bring to a boil over high heat, stirring once with a fork. Reduce heat. Cover and simmer for 12 to 14 minutes, or until all liquid is absorbed.

A Gift of Grains

Package Arie's Herb and Rice Mix in a pretty jar for an unusual gift that is not expensive. You can use plain white rice or a specialty rice. Many varieties of rice — such as basmati, jasmine, and wild rice mixtures — are available in bulk at natural food and gourmet stores.

All-Soup Seasoning

*Judy Kehs of **Cricket Hill Herb Farm** says, "We use this blend liberally in just about every soup except chowders. It is very good in post-Thanksgiving leftover turkey soups. The touch of lemon may seem like an odd ingredient, but it enhances the other good flavors in the soup without actually being detectable as lemon flavoring. This very serviceable blend can even rescue a bland commercial soup!"*

YIELD: ½ CUP

  2 tablespoons dried parsley
  1 tablespoon dried thyme
  ½ tablespoon dried chervil
  ½ tablespoon dried basil
  ½ tablespoon dried marjoram
  ½ tablespoon celery seed
  1 teaspoon dried savory (summer or winter)
  1 teaspoon dried rosemary
  1 teaspoon dried lemon zest

Mix all herbs thoroughly and store in an airtight container away from heat and light.

Variations. Substitute 2 tablespoons lemon thyme for plain thyme and lemon zest. Add about 5 juniper berries to beef soups for a special tang.

Suggested Uses

 Season any homemade soup (beef, vegetable, or poultry) to taste, or use approximately 1 tablespoon of the herb blend to 1 quart of stock. Use the blend also in hearty stews and for Swiss steak and meat sauces.

Cricket Hill Herb Farm
Rowley, Massachusetts

When developing their specialty herb blends, Cricket Hill tries for "ones with wide applications rather than those limited to use in just one dish," says owner Judy Kehs. A fun part of blending, she notes, is having a wide range of herbs to choose from. "Discover some of the special herbs, such as celery-flavored lovage, delightful lemon thyme, garlic chives, and unusual basils such as Thai, lemon, and tangy Mexican," Judy urges herb growers. "The basils are annuals, but the others are hardy perennials — even in New England — and continue to produce for many more years."

Cricket Hill Herb Farm
Rowley, Massachusetts

Owner Judy Kehs has been growing and selling herbs for nearly twenty years. She grows over three hundred common and uncommon herbs, and lectures on the history, culture, and uses of herbs. She notes that the use of herbs can "turn a simple basic dish into something very special as well as healthful," as with this recipe for perking up zucchini. Judy says that Cricket Hill's own experience in developing blends is that they evolve over time, after much experimentation in the kitchen. "Quite honestly, it took unsuccessful as well as successful experiments to create blends that we were satisfied with," she says. "So don't be afraid to experiment!"

Zesty Zucchini Seasoning

*This blend was created at **Cricket Hill Herb Farm** out of desperation — "to help us survive and consume a typically overwhelming crop of zucchini. We have enjoyed it in soups, salads, casseroles, vegetable stir fries, and more," says Judy Kehs. "Our customers report it's good in pasta sauces with tomatoes, as well."*

YIELD: ABOUT ¾ CUP

> 8 tablespoons dried parsley
> 4 tablespoons dried chives
> 1 teaspoon dried marjoram
> 1 teaspoon dried oregano
> 1 teaspoon dried thyme
> 1 teaspoon dried basil
> ½ teaspoon celery seed

Combine all ingredients and mix well. The blend should be stored in a sealed container and kept away from heat and light.

Suggested Uses

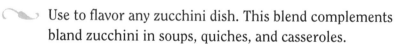

- Use to flavor any zucchini dish. This blend complements bland zucchini in soups, quiches, and casseroles.
- Mix with crumbs to make breaded sliced zucchini or zucchini fingers.
- This is an excellent seasoning on summer squash and tomato dishes and sauces. It is a very versatile and helpful blend to have on hand at the end of summer when fresh zucchini, summer squash, and garden tomatoes are readily available. Experiment and enjoy!
- In the summer, make this blend with fresh herbs (along with dried celery seed), toss thinly sliced fresh zucchini and add to a salad of greens and tomato wedges. Serve with a vinaigrette dressing.

Quick Vegetable Dish

Zucchini, thinly sliced
Summer squash, thinly sliced
Onion, thinly sliced
Celery, thinly sliced
Water
1 bouillon cube (vegetable, chicken or beef)
Parmesan cheese
Zesty Zucchini Seasoning, to taste

Simmer desired quantity of sliced vegetables in water with bouillon cube until tender. Drain, toss with cheese and Zesty Zucchini Seasoning. Serve hot.

CHAPTER 8

BREAD AND DESSERT BLENDS

Herb and spice mixtures make food special, particularly when it comes to dessert. You will find many ideas here for holiday fare — from pumpkin dip and pumpkin ice cream dessert to holiday cookies and special tea cakes.

A number of the blend recipes in this chapter take off from the basic "mixed spices" blend you find in the grocery store — cinnamon, ginger, cloves, and nutmeg — and give it an unusual twist by combining it with other flavors or suggesting different ways to use a mixed spices blend besides the traditional pumpkin pie. These recipes revisit and expand the taste possibilities of mixed spices.

The addition of lemon zest or orange zest is a great way to brighten up the flavor of mixed spices. These blends are great in fruit pies and fruit compotes, which can be made with either canned fruit or dried fruit cooked in a port wine with the spice mix. Pears cooked in red wine and one of these spice mixtures is another elegant yet easy dessert you may want to try. These baking mixtures also make great additions to crumbled toppings for muffins or fruit.

Many of the serving suggestions in this chapter also make great holiday gifts, from pie-spiced nuts to lavender cookies.

Cricket Hill Herb Farm
Rowley, Massachusetts

Cricket Hill Herb Farm opened in 1976, the year of the U.S. bicentennial celebration. "This seemed an appropriate time to launch an herb business in an area settled in 1630, when herbs were so very much a part of the lifestyle," notes owner Judy Kehs. Nearly twenty years old now, the business is thriving with sales of over three hundred varieties of herbs grown in greenhouses and outdoors, their own culinary blends, teas, books, and crafts. Customers enjoy browsing in the farm's display gardens, and Judy is pleased to say that as a result of their years of success, the staff is able to help and advise customers on all aspects of herb growing and use.

Pumpkin Pie Spices

This version of a classic spice combination comes from Cricket Hill Herb Farm.

YIELD: ABOUT ½ CUP

- 5 tablespoons ground cinnamon
- 4 teaspoons ground ginger
- 2 teaspoons ground cloves
- 2 teaspoons ground nutmeg
- 2 teaspoons ground allspice

Mix to blend and store in airtight containers away from heat and light.

Pumpkin Pie–Spiced Nuts

"This is such a simple recipe that even a child can make it," says Judy Kehs of **Cricket Hill Herb Farm.** *"My eight-year-old son made several batches of Pumpkin Pie–Spiced Nuts one Christmas, put them in pretty jars, and gave them as gifts. They were such a hit that he has been doing it ever since (he is now in his twenties). Besides gift-giving, these nuts are always well received as a party snack. At the farm we serve them in the fall to guests along with our own homemade cider."*

YIELD: 4½ CUPS

One 8-ounce jar dry-roasted peanuts
 ½ cup pecans
 ½ cup walnut halves
 1 egg, lightly beaten
 1 teaspoon water
 ¾ cup sugar
 1 tablespoon Pumpkin Pie Spices
 ¾ teaspoon salt

Combine the nuts. Mix together the egg and water, and toss with the nut mixture. Combine the sugar, Pumpkin Pie Spices, and salt, and toss that with the nuts until they are well coated. Spread nuts in a single layer on a lightly greased cookie sheet. Bake at 300°F for 20 to 25 minutes. Break up any large clusters and allow to cool.

Variation. Other combinations of nuts can be used. Try almonds instead of pecans, if desired.

Dry Creek Herb Farm and
Learning Center
Auburn, California

Shatoiya and Rick de la Tour began
their herbal venture with a learning
center established in 1988 in the
Sierra Foothills near Sacramento,
California. Shatoiya is a flower essence
and herbal therapist, known
internationally for her teaching and
lecturing. In 1990, they opened their
gardens to the public and established a
Victorian gift shop with an herbal
apothecary and an herb plant nursery.
A Mongolian yurt makes an unusual
classroom.

Dry Creek Herb Farm Pumpkin Pie Spice

*Shatoiya and Rick de la Tour of **Dry Creek Herb Farm and Learning Center** developed this zesty version of pumpkin pie spice.*

YIELD: 1½ CUPS

½ cup cinnamon chips*
¼ cup whole star anise
⅛ cup fennel seeds
⅛ cup dried orange peel
⅛ cup whole cloves
⅛ cup dried ginger

*To make cinnamon chips, crush whole cinnamon sticks with a hammer or other heavy object.

Grind all the ingredients until powdered in a spice grinder. Be sure to stop grinding intermittently to keep the herbs from overheating. Most of the flavor in herbs and spices comes from their volatile oils, which can be destroyed by excessive heat. Store in an airtight glass container away from heat and light.

Suggested Uses

 Adds delicious flavor to cakes, muffins, cookies, and pies.
 This spice blend can also be added to ground coffee before brewing to add a zesty taste.
For pumpkin pie, add 1½ teaspoons spice blend for a mild flavor, or up to 1 tablespoon for a stronger flavor.

Shatoiya's Famous Holiday Cookies

YIELD: 3 DOZEN COOKIES

1	cup butter
2	cups brown sugar
2	eggs
2	teaspoons vanilla extract
2	cups unbleached flour
2½	cups oatmeal
1	teaspoon baking soda
1	heaping tablespoon Dry Creek Herb Farm Pumpkin Pie Spice
1	teaspoon baking powder
½	teaspoon salt
1	cup chopped walnuts
12	ounces butterscotch chips (optional)

Blend together the butter and brown sugar. Add the eggs and vanilla extract. To this add the flour, oatmeal, soda, Dry Creek Herb Farm Pumpkin Pie Spice, baking powder, and salt, and blend. Add walnuts and butterscotch chips. Roll into small balls. Place about 2 inches apart on a greased cookie sheet. Bake for 10 minutes at 375°F.

Rose Manor Bed & Breakfast
Manheim, Pennsylvania

Susan Jenal offers everything from herbal pet care products to teas, vinegars, potpourri, and everlasting arrangements in her gift shop. Overnight guests and shop visitors can enjoy the manor's herb and rose gardens, as well.

Spicy Baking Mixture

This versatile baking spice blend comes from Rose Manor Bed & Breakfast.

YIELD: ABOUT ⅓ CUP

> 2 tablespoons ground cinnamon
> 1 tablespoon lemon peel powder
> 1 tablespoon ground cloves
> 1½ teaspoons ground ginger
> 1½ teaspoons ground nutmeg

Mix ingredients together and store in airtight glass container away from heat and light.

Suggested Uses

 For pumpkin pie: Add 1¾ teaspoons Spicy Baking Mixture per 2 cups canned pumpkin.

 For apple pie: Use 1 teaspoon Spicy Baking Mixture per 6 cups of thinly sliced tart apples.

For spiced fruit compote: In a frying pan, melt ⅓ cup butter. Add ¾ cup firmly packed brown sugar and ½ teaspoon Spicy Baking Mixture. Add 6 cups drained canned peaches, pears, and pineapple chunks. Cover and simmer 10 to 15 minutes, stirring occasionally. Serve warm.

 For streusel-topped muffins: Combine ¼ cup firmly packed brown sugar, 2 tablespoons softened butter, 1 tablespoon flour, and ½ teaspoon Spicy Baking Mixture. Sprinkle over muffin batter in baking pan and bake as directed. This is a tasty topping for plain muffins, applesauce muffins, pumpkin muffins, or apple-cinnamon muffins.

Mexican Cinnamon Sugar Topping

Woodland Herbs created this sweet topping mix.

YIELD: 1⅛ CUPS

> 1 cup sugar
> 1 tablespoon ground cinnamon
> 1 tablespoon cocoa

Combine the sugar, cinnamon, and cocoa and mix thoroughly.

Suggested Uses

 Use on warm puddings, custards, oatmeal, and sugar cookies.

Sweet Spice Blend

Here's another way of spicing up your sweets from Woodland Herbs.

YIELD: ABOUT ⅓ CUP

> 1 tablespoon orange peel powder
> 1 tablespoon ground nutmeg
> 1 tablespoon ground cloves
> 1 tablespoon ground ginger
> 2 tablespoons ground cinnamon

Mix thoroughly to blend.

Suggested Uses

 Stir spice blend into ice cream, yogurt, fruit, oatmeal, or add 2 to 3 tablespoons to cake or quick bread batters.

Woodland Herbs
Northport, Michigan

Located in a valley surrounded by hills and sugar maples, Woodland Herbs is the oldest and largest herb farm in northern Michigan. Owner Pat Bourdo sells hard-to-find herbs and spices, salt-free dips and blends, herbal candies, vinegars, and condiments from her culinary herb shop. The grounds also include a display garden that is open to the public in season.

Prairie Trail Farm
Goshen, Indiana

Prairie Trail Farm's retail shop, called The Secret Garden, specializes in growing herbs and flowers for the dried floral arrangements they design and make. Owner Renee Troyer Campbell also does custom drying for special occasions and memory wreaths.

Pumpkin Dip

YIELD: 3–4 CUPS

2 cups powdered sugar
One 8-ounce package
    cream cheese
One 15-ounce can
    pumpkin purée
1½ teaspoons Prairie
    Trail Farm Pumpkin
    Pie Spice

Combine sugar and cream cheese until well blended. Beat in remaining ingredients. Store in refrigerator. Serve in a small hollowed-out pumpkin with gingersnaps.

Prairie Trail Farm Pumpkin Pie Spice

*Renee Troyer Campbell of **Prairie Trail Farm** developed this recipe by adapting a recipe her aunt used to make.*

YIELD: ABOUT ⅓ CUP

3 tablespoons ground cinnamon
3 teaspoons ground nutmeg
1½ teaspoons ground ginger
1½ teaspoons ground cloves

Mix spices thoroughly to blend, and store in an airtight container.

Pumpkin Ice Cream Dessert

YIELD: ONE 9 BY 13-INCH PIE

2¾ cups graham cracker crumbs
½ cup melted butter or margarine
2 tablespoons sugar
2 cups pumpkin purée
1¼ to 1½ cups sugar
4 teaspoons Prairie Trail Farm Pumpkin Pie Spice
½ gallon vanilla ice cream, softened

Mix together the cracker crumbs, melted butter or margarine, and 2 tablespoons sugar. Reserve ½ cup for topping. Press remainder into a 9 by 13-inch pan. Blend together the pumpkin, remaining sugar, Prairie Trail Farm Pumpkin Pie Spice, and softened ice cream. Pour over crumb crust. Sprinkle remaining crumbs over the top. Freeze for several hours before serving.

Mixed Spice Blend

The Rosemary House says, "We got the recipe from a group of church cooks who burned their mortgage by holding bake sales and offering the best apple cake in the world. This spice blend was their secret ingredient."

YIELD: ABOUT ½ CUP

      6 teaspoons ground coriander
      5 teaspoons ground cinnamon
      4 teaspoons ground allspice
      3 teaspoons ground nutmeg
      2 teaspoons ground ginger
      1 teaspoon ground cloves

Mix all spices thoroughly and keep in airtight container away from heat and light.

Variation. Store spice blend in a lidded jar with a whole vanilla bean that's been slit so that the flavors blend smoothly.

Suggested Uses

This superb blend is useful wherever a recipe calls for mixed spices — apple pie, fruit cake, baked fruits, spiced cookies, tea breads, and so on. We use this all the time instead of having to carefully measure a bit of this and a hint of that.

The Rosemary House, Inc.
Mechanicsburg, Pennsylvania

The Rosemary House is truly a family affair. Susanna Reppert is manager of the shop, following in the footsteps of her mother, and founder of the shop, Bertha Reppert. Susanna is a master gardener and author of a booklet on "Kitchen Cosmetics."

The Rosemary House stocks fresh and dried herbs and spices, seeds, and plants, as well as a wide array of herbal products. The building is bordered by herb gardens, including an eighteenth-century garden where visitors can relax and enjoy the fragrances.

Herb Society of Palm Beach County
West Palm Beach, Florida

Attesting to the fact that what you grow depends on the climate you live in, the Herb Society of Palm Beach County specializes in tropical herbs. Living in subtropic Florida, says member Carolyn Henbenstreit Smith, "I have a gigantic rosemary bush, that is in bloom nine months a year outdoors, but I must grow garlic chives instead of regular chives since they are hardier in a hot climate." Noting the growing challenges she faces with the other herbs in this blend recipe, Smith says, "I often have to replace or dry parsley and sage, which do not survive long in our summer rains."

The Herb Society sponsors an annual "Herbal Fantasy" featuring two days of lectures, seminars, luncheons, and herb plant sales. They also help maintain a subtropical herb garden at the Mounts Botanical Garden in West Palm Beach.

Herb Bread Blend

The Herb Society of Palm Beach County offers this do-it-yourself alternative to buying costly loaves of specialty herb bread.

YIELD: ⅔ CUP

- 4 tablespoons dried rosemary
- 4 tablespoons dried sage
- 4 teaspoons dried Italian (flat-leaf) parsley
- 4 teaspoons dried chives

Combine all ingredients and mix well. Store in airtight container away from heat and light.

Variation. Add freshly grated Parmesan, cheddar, or gruyere cheese to blend before combining with bread dough. In season, try making this blend with fresh herbs, increasing quantities by ⅓ to ½.

Suggested Uses

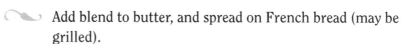

- Add blend to butter, and spread on French bread (may be grilled).
- For herb bread, add 3½ tablespoons of blend to a standard bread recipe.
- Add blend to soda bread, bread stuffings, scones, biscuits, cheese twists, and focaccia.

Herbal Flower Mix

Dried herbal flowers add a delicate taste and a pretty touch to desserts in this mix suggestion from Richland Creek Herb Farm.

½ cup dried lavender flowers or dried rose geranium leaves

Place dried lavender flowers or rose geranium leaves in a blender and chop until fine. Store in glass jars.

Suggested Uses

- **For lavender or rose geranium cake:** Add 3 tablespoons herbal flower mix to any white or yellow cake mix, or to a plain cake recipe.
- **For lavender or rose geranium cookies:** Add 3 tablespoons herbal flower mix to any plain cookie recipe.
- **For lavender or rose geranium iced tea:** Put 3 tablespoons herbal flower mix and 3 regular tea bags in a coffee filter. Place in coffee maker and add water for a full pot. If you don't want to use coffee maker, place mix and tea bags in large tea pot and add hot water. Transfer tea to a gallon pitcher or container, add 1 cup sugar, and serve over ice.

Richland Creek Herb Farm
Seagrove, North Carolina

From their farm in the center of North Carolina, the Britt family produces 300 varieties of herbs, more than any other herb farm in the state. At their annual Herbfest, they serve hundreds of people. "Many people are amazed at how simple it is to make a very elegant cake, cookies, and tea with herbs," says Rebecca Britt. "You can add all kinds of different herbs, but of all the combinations we have tried over the years, these two simple additions — lavender flowers or rose geranium leaves — are the favorites of our Herbfest guests."

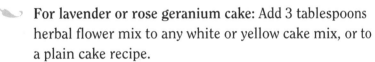

Drying Lavender and Rose Geranium

If you grow lavender or rose geraniums, you can dry the plants needed for this recipe. For lavender, bundle the stems with a rubber band and hang to dry. When dry, remove the dried flowers from the stem. For rose geranium, pick the leaves off the plant and lay them in a shallow box to dry. When dry, remove as much of the stem as possible.

CHAPTER 9

HERBAL TEAS AND BEVERAGES

erbal tea blends are fun to make because there are so many possibilities — and they're easy and inexpensive to make at home. It's easy to experiment with herbal flowers and many edible flowers, as well.

You can create a tea blend with your favorite flavors, or a blend with great health benefits, a blend to wake you up, another to help you sleep, a blend to make you happy, and another that's just a wonderful way to drink tea. Personalized blends to meet the needs and tastes of friends make great gifts, too. Just pack a tin of tea in a pretty teapot or handmade tea cozy and you've got a beautiful, warming gift.

The spice blends for cider in this chapter show how many different taste variations you can get on an old-favorite combination of spices. These blends don't need to be limited to cider and wine, either. There are many flavored juices available today that would taste great warmed with mulled spices.

Village Herb Shop
Blue Ball, Pennsylvania

Based in Lancaster County, Pennsylvania, the Village Herb Shop shares quarters with several other business in a renovated tobacco packinghouse dating from 1911. Owner Patrice Dyer notes that they began with an unusual location and sought to complement this with a line of unusual and clever herbal products and accessories not carried elsewhere. The staff also prides itself on being knowledgeable about all aspects of herbs — from plant problems and identification to using herbs and oils for food, cosmetic, and health purposes — and able to really serve the customers.

Wassail Spice Mix

*Patrice Dyer of the **Village Herb Shop** says, "This recipe has evolved and gotten better as we've run out of ingredients and had to substitute other ingredients we had in stock. We were not prepared for the popular response to the package we came up with containing a batch of the Wassail Spice Mix, a punch recipe, and a muslin bag. People love this quick, easy way to make a holiday beverage, and it makes an inexpensive party favor as well. Add a bottle of wine, and you have an excellent host/hostess gift."*

YIELD: 1 BAG (ENOUGH FOR FLAVORING 2 PUNCH BOWLS)

Four 3-inch cinnamon sticks
   9 whole cloves
   3 medium pieces of crystallized ginger
   6 cardamom pods
  ½ cup candied or dried orange peel

Combine all ingredients in a small muslin bag. Store bag in an airtight container until ready to use.

Variation. Use three small pieces dried whole gingerroot instead of crystallized ginger.

Suggested Uses

 For steaming wassail punch bowl: In a large pan, place one bag Wassail Spice Mix, 1 cup raisins, and 1½ quarts grape juice (or 1 quart wine); bring to the simmering point. Simmer for one hour. Remove spice bag (it can be reused one more time). Add 1 gallon cider, and heat just long enough to bring the mixture to a simmer. Pour into a preheated punch bowl and serve. When the punch is all gone, the raisins may be eaten — they are really tasty after soaking in the brew. Wassail gets better with age, so make it ahead of time and reheat.

For a variation replace the cider with 1 or 1½ gallons cranapple juice, which won't get frothy or separate the way cider can when it gets too hot and is a prettier color than cider.

Drying Orange Peel

Patrice Dyer, who developed this recipe, suggests drying your own orange peel for the best flavor. Wash the orange, remove the skin with a vegetable peeler (leaving the white part on the orange), and air-dry the peel on paper towels.

Earthshine Herb & Book Shop
Monson, Massachusetts

Owner Debbie Rose Hayes began Earthshine Herb & Book Shop out of a desire to make a living doing what she loves, and to share her love of herbs with more people. Teaching workshops and sharing information informally with customers are two of her favorite activities. Besides the culinary aspect of herbs, Debbie is interested in alternative ways of treating physical and emotional problems with herbs. Her shop features a book section that covers the many aspects of using herbs. Earthshine extends its educational component further with a rental section of audio and video casettes on herb and self-improvement related topics.

Mulling Spices

*Debbie Rose Hayes of **Earthshine Herb & Book Shop** developed this warm and tasty mixture for fall and winter gatherings. "The extra benefit is the aroma that will fill your home," says Debbie.*

YIELD: 4½ CUPS

> 1½ cups cinnamon chips*
> 1½ cups dried chopped orange peel
> 1 cup whole allspice berries
> ½ cup whole cloves

*To make cinnamon chips, crush whole cinnamon sticks with a hammer or other heavy object.

Mix ingredients thoroughly and store in an airtight jar.

Suggested Uses

Use ¼ cup of Mulling Spices per half gallon of cider, apple juice, or wine. Simmer for ½ hour before serving.

A Gift of Wassail

Pack a small muslin bag with mulling spices into a glass-footed mug and tie on a big red ribbon to take to your holiday-party host and hostess. You can also combine the spices with a special holiday mug or a bottle of wine.

Old Time Mulled Cider Spice

Rainbow's End Herbs reports that their version of mulled spices "is a hit everytime." Jacqueline Swift says, "We have found that leftover mulled cider will keep for weeks in the refrigerator and will not turn. It tastes great as a cold beverage or can be reheated."

YIELD: ENOUGH FOR 1 QUART CIDER

   2 cinnamon sticks
12 whole cloves
   7 whole allspice berries
   2 star anise
   1 tablespoon dried orange zest

Mix spices together.

Suggested Use

 To make mulled cider, add the spices to 1 quart sweet cider. Bring to a boil in a glass, stainless, or enameled pan. Strain. Serve hot, garnished with orange slices. Serves 5.

Rainbow's End Herbs
Perrysburg, New York

Rainbow's End Herbs is located in western New York State, high in the hills overlooking Lake Erie. The forty-acre farm houses farm animals and nature trails, as well as herb and organic vegetable gardens. Owner Jacqueline Swift offers a variety of educational programs, including wild-plant walks and classes for children. She serves this cider to the farm's visitors. "If I have leftover cider mix at the end of the season," she notes, "I add a few drops of Harvest Apple potpourri scent to it and use it for a simmering potpourri."

Thyme & Seasons Books
Bertram, Texas

True to their Texas roots, Thyme &
Seasons Books specializes in using the
traditional spices and flavors of the
Southwest in their herb mixes, right
down to their hot chocolate.

South of the Border Hot Chocolate Mix

*Thyme & Seasons Books created this hot chocolate
blend — Texas-style!*

YIELD: ABOUT ¾ CUP (ENOUGH TO MAKE 6 SERVINGS)

- ½ cup sugar
- 1 tablespoon flour
- ¼ cup cocoa
- ¼ teaspoon salt
- 1 teaspoon ground cinnamon
- ¾ teaspoon ground cloves
- ⅛ teaspoon ground allspice

Blend all ingredients thoroughly.

Suggested Use

 To make hot chocolate, add ¾ cup mix to 2 cups water
and simmer for 4 minutes. Stir in 6 cups milk and
reheat. Add 1 teaspoon vanilla, whip, and serve.

Herbed Ice Cubes

"It's wonderful to enjoy the taste of fresh herbs in these ice cubes in the midst of winter!" says Julie Bailey of **Mountain Rose Herbs**. *"Add them to a tall-stemmed glass of water for a simple, dramatic, fragrant, and beautiful experience."*

Fresh borage flowers
Fresh rose petals
Fresh thyme flowers
Fresh sage flowers
Fresh nasturtium flowers
Fresh rose geranium leaves
Fresh rosemary flowers
Fresh bee balm flowers
Fresh lavender flowers
Fresh calendula flowers
Fresh chamomile flowers

Mix and match herbs, according to your eye and nose. Place selected herbs in ice cube trays, add water, and freeze. Transfer ice cubes to a closed (and labeled) container when frozen, and keep in freezer until ready to use.

Variation. Use basil, lemon balm, or any combination of edible flowers.

Suggested Uses

 Serve in a tall glass with iced tea, fruit juice, white wine, or sparkling water.

Mountain Rose Herbs
Redway, California

A home-based business in the coastal mountains of northern California, Mountain Rose Herbs is committed to conserving resources and "living lightly on the earth." They use all recyled packaging (collected regularly from local businesses) for their array of high-quality organic herbs and supplies for herbalists. Their products are featured in their publication, "The Catalogue of Herbal Delights," issued twice a year.

Herbs etc
Barrington, Rhode Island

Located halfway between Providence and Newport, Rhode Island, Herbs etc strives to be a peaceful, soothing place for "harried" customers to relax and unwind. Owner Jill Bradfur is especially interested in the horticultural aspects of cultivating herbs. She sells plants, topiary, books, jewelry, and garden ornaments, and has gardens that are open to the public.

Rest Easy Tea Blend

Herbs etc created this combination of herbs especially for relief after a stressful day.

YIELD: 2¾ CUPS

¼ cup dried spearmint
¼ cup dried lemongrass
1 cup dried lemon balm
½ cup dried catnip
¾ cup dried chamomile flowers

Blend all herbs thoroughly and store in an airtight container away from heat and light.

Suggested Use

 To make tea, use 2 teaspoons of blend for each cup of boiling water.

Calming Spirit Tea Blend

*This very tasty tea from **Tea & Herb Essence** is wonderful iced or hot, says Laureen Grenus. These herbs are traditionally used to calm the nerves, settle the stomach, and uplift. Other herbs can be added, as desired.*

YIELD: ABOUT 4 CUPS (RECIPE CAN BE CUT IN HALF FOR SMALLER PORTION)

> 1 cup dried rosemary leaves
> 1 cup dried lavender flowers
> 1 cup dried spearmint
> ½ cup dried chamomile
> ¼ to ½ cup dried cloves

Blend all herbs thoroughly and store in an airtight container away from heat and light.

Suggested Uses

- To make tea, use one teaspoon of loose herbs per cup of water. You can prepare the tea in a tea ball, or mix the loose herbs with water in a tea pot and then strain tea into a cup.
- Place a handful of herbs in a muslin bag and add bag to your bathwater for a soothing treat.

Tea & Herb Essence
Newport, Rhode Island

Located along the waterfront in coastal Newport, Tea & Herb Essence specializes in medicinal herbs, teas, candles, and aromatherapy products. Owner and herbalist Laureen Grenus blends twenty varieties of loose leaf herbal teas on the premises. The shop also has floral herb display gardens that are open to the public. Laureen offers lectures and workshops year-round.

Victorian Herb Gardens
Cattaraugus, New York

Located high in the hills of western New York State, the Victorian Herb Gardens offer visitors a range of nature experiences — from woodland gardens to large formal display and antique rose gardens in full sunshine to an English cottage garden and a chamomile lawn — all with an outstanding view. Visitors are encouraged to bring a picnic lunch and enjoy the peaceful setting. Owner Peggy Filock established the business in 1992 after the local hospital where she had worked as a music therapist for fifteen years closed. Peggy says she enjoys "combining the business of herbs and the art of gardening with music and the visual arts (through garden design and the use of color and texture)."

"Signature Blend" Herbal Tea

"This was my first attempt at blending my own tea," says Peggy Filock of **Victorian Herb Gardens,** *"and it has remained one of our favorites and a best-seller."*

YIELD: 3½ CUPS

> 1 cup dried pineapple sage
> 1 cup dried chamomile flowers
> 1 cup dried rosehips
> ½ cup dried lemon balm

Blend all herbs thoroughly and store in an airtight container.

Variation. This tea can also be made with fresh herbs.

Suggested Use

 To make tea, use one teaspoon of herbs per cup of water. Tea is delicious either hot or cold. If serving as an iced tea, garnish with fresh pineapple sage flowers.

Quiet Time Herb Tea Blend

"All the herbs in this recipe can be found growing wild in most of the United States," says Jane Esotelle of *Underwood Herbs*.

YIELD: 2¾ CUPS

> 1 cup dried chamomile flowers
> 1 cup dried strawberry leaves
> ½ cup dried catnip leaves
> ¼ cup dried thyme

Crush herbs before measuring. Combine and blend well.

Suggested Use

 To make tea, pour 1 cup boiling water over 1 teaspoon tea blend. Let steep 5 to 10 minutes. This blend contains no caffeine, making it a good bedtime tea.

Iron Tonic Herb Tea Blend

This tea from Underwood Herbs helps increase iron in the blood.

YIELD: 2½ CUPS

> 1 cup dried mullein leaves
> 1 cup dried stinging nettle leaves
> ¼ cup dried strawberry leaves
> ¼ cup dried red clover blossoms

Crush herbs before measuring. Combine and blend well. To make tea, pour 1 cup boiling water over 1 teaspoon tea blend. Let steep 5 to 10 minutes.

Underwood Herbs
Chateaugay, New York

Jane Esotelle began her business in 1978 by selling herb teas blended from herbs found wild in the Adirondack Mountains. She continues to make most of her products from plants found wild in the woods and meadows of the Adirondacks, and leads wild food and medicinal plant walks. In the course of a two-hour walk along country dirt roads, participants learn to identify and use plants found along the way. Jane has also published several books, including *How to Use Herbs and Spices* and, most recently, *Wild Herb Teas of Northern New York.* These recipes come from the latter book.

Captain Morgan's Herbs
North, Virginia

Owner Wendy Wells sells herb plants, herbal body care products, books, and gifts from her greenhouse and farm, Captain Morgan's Herbs, and her gift shop, The Captain's Lady. The company also has a mail-order catalog that was started to meet customers' demands to obtain their hand-milled lavender soap. These handmade, hand-cut soaps are still featured, along with many other herb products.

Wendy also conducts workshops on making herbal topiaries and wreaths and herbal medicines. Additionally, she teaches the Virginia Master Gardener classes on herbs in nearby districts and is a regular lecturer at garden clubs, schools, libraries, and other groups.

Sweet Dreams Tea Blend

*Wendy Wells, owner of **Captain Morgan's Herbs**, says, "This tea was formulated at the request of a friend for her insomnia. The orange peel and cloves were added to make it a bit more palatable, as some people find the taste of valerian a little strong. Three years later I still blend my friend's tea for her, but advise her to not use it nightly for any length of time since the effectiveness of the herbs decreases with prolonged use. It's good to take a 2 to 3 week break after several months of regular use for treating insomnia."*

YIELD: 2⅓ CUPS

- 3 tablespoons ground valerian root
- ½ cup dried peppermint
- ½ cup dried scullcap
- ½ cup dried lemon balm
- ½ cup dried passion flower
- Dried orange peel and whole cloves (optional)

Mix ingredients well, and store in an airtight glass jar.

Suggested Use

 Infuse as a tea in a covered vessel, using 1 heaping tablespoon of blend per 1 cup of boiling water. Steep for 15 minutes. Sweeten with honey, if desired.

Good Health Tea Blend

*Denice Suhay of **Weaver Creek Herbs** says, "I really enjoy drinking this tea. It is cleansing, nutritive, and promotes overall health. It seems to make everything in the body work right and flow freely. Try it, and I am sure you will love it as I do."*

YIELD: 1¼ CUPS

- 3 tablespoons dried red raspberry leaves
- 3 tablespoons dried peppermint
- 2 tablespoons dried red clover flowers
- 2 tablespoons dried dandelion leaves
- 2 tablespoons dried nettle leaves
- 2 tablespoons dried cleavers
- 2 tablespoons dried ephedra
- 2 tablespoons dried ginkgo leaves
- 1 tablespoon dried oatstraw

Mix all herbs thoroughly and store in an airtight jar away from heat and light.

Suggested Use

 For tea, boil 2 quarts water, remove from stove, and add 2 muslin bags with 8 tablespoons of Good Health Tea Blend in each bag. Cover and steep for about 30 minutes. Add 2 more quarts hot water, making 1 gallon of tea.

Weaver Creek Herbs
Weaverville, California

The mother/daughter team of Denice Suhay and Connie Loretz started their business in 1994 to bring herbs and supplies to the small mountain town of Weaverville. They were inspired by the plentitude of wild herbs available right around them and by their enjoyment of wild crafting — gathering wild herbs — for making tea. The walkway to their small shop is filled with exotic herbs that entice people into the store. Weaver Creek Herbs specializes in helping people make their own herbal products, medicinals, and cosmetics.

Walk In Beauty
Colfax, California

Owner Kathy Lee places a special emphasis on the health benefits of herbs and the ways in which herbs can increase both the flavor and nutritional value of foods. She emphasizes that each person should tailor recipes to fit their individual needs. Kathy teaches numerous herb classes, including one on Herbal Remedies for Arthritis.

High Calcium Tea Blend

*This blend from **Walk In Beauty** contains chamomile, which is high in calcium and has anti-inflammatory properties. Owner Kathy Lee says that anyone with allergies to ragweed may want to eliminate the chamomile in this recipe. For those growing their own herbs, she advises that nettle and horsetail can both be invasive in wet areas, so you may want to plant them in a contained area of the garden.*

YIELD: 1¼ CUPS

    2 ounces dried nettle leaves
    2 ounces dried oatstraw
    2 ounces dried chamomile flowers
    1 ounce dried alfalfa
    1 ounce dried horsetail
    1 ounce dried red raspberry leaves
    1 ounce dried spearmint (or more to taste)

Mix up dry herb tea blend and store in an airtight glass jar away from heat and light.

Suggested Use

 To prepare tea, use one teaspoon per cup of boiling water and infuse (covered) for 10 minutes.

SUPPLIERS

Recipe Contributors/Mail-Order Suppliers

Most of the herb business who have contributed recipes to this collection sell bulk herbs at their shop and through a mail-order catalog. Find a shop near you and call or write them for purchasing or ordering information. Send a stamped, self-addressed envelope to the businesses listing a SASE. (See state-by-state listing on page 143).

Arie's Herb Gardens
300 Pineview Road
Sylacauga, Alabama 35150
(205) 249-8199
Garden open to public. Wholesale; retail. Mail/phone order.

Becker's Cottage Garden Herb Farm
1118 Killian Road
Akron, Ohio 44312
(216) 644-3408
Garden open to public. Wholesale; retail.

Bittersweet Herb Farm
RR 1, Box 166, Laurel Lane
Charlemont, Massachusetts 01339
(413) 339-8311
Wholesale; retail. Mail/phone order. Free catalog.

Broadacres Herbs
RR 1, Box 2065
South China, Maine 04358
(207) 445-2779
Wholesale. Mail/phone order. Catalog, SASE

Captain Morgan's Herbs
PO Box 306, Route 617
North, Virginia 23128
(804) 725-5744
Retail. Mail/phone order. Catalog $1.

Clement Herb Farm
19690 Clement's Lane
Rogers, Arkansas 72756
(501) 925-1603
Garden open to public. Wholesale, retail. Mail/phone order. Catalog $1.

Cricket Hill Herb Farm
74 Glen Street
Rowley, Massachusetts 01969
(508) 948-2818
Garden open to public. Retail.

Devonshire Apothecary
PO Box 160215
Austin, Texas 78716-0215
(512) 477-8270

Dry Creek Herb Farm and Learning Center
13935 Dry Creek Road
Auburn, California 95602
(916) 878-2441
Gardens open to public. Wholesale (line of organic herbal skin care products); retail (Victorian Gift Shop). Mail/phone order. Catalog $2 (refundable with purchase).

Earthshine Herb & Book Shop
14 Maple Street
Monson, Massachusetts 01057
(413) 267-9062
Book section, alternative video and audio rental section; workshops.

Elderflower Farm
501 Callahan Road
Roseburg, Oregon 97470
(503) 672-9803
Garden open to public (by appointment). Wholesale; retail. Mail/phone order. Catalog $1.

Frog Park Herbs
455 Frog Park Road
Waterville, NY 13480
(315) 841-8636
Garden open to public, seasonally. Retail. Mail/phone order. Catalog.

Goldenrod Mountain Herbs
240 Wildcat Road
Deep Gap, North Carolina 28618
(704) 264-2683
Garden open to public (by appointment). Wholesale, retail. Mail/phone order.

Good Thyme Farm
Route 132, Kasson Road
Bethlehem, Connecticut 06751
(203) 266-5265
Garden open to public (by appointment). Wholesale. Mail/phone order. Catalog $1.

The Herb Market
Jail and Green Streest
Washington, Kentucky 41096
(606) 759-7815; Fax: (606) 759-5745
Garden open to public. Wholesale; retail. Mail/phone order. Catalog $3.50.

Herb Society of Palm Beach County
531 N. Military Trail
West Palm Beach, Florida 33462
Garden open to public.

Herbal Essence
7116 E. Mercer
Scottsdale, Arizona 85254
(602) 948-6073
Retail. Mail/phone order. Catalog.

Herbal Lakes
6015 Parkland Drive
Chagrin Falls, Ohio 44022
(216)-338-7113
Retail (by appointment).

Herbs etc
19 West Street
Barrington, Rhode Island 02806
(401) 245-9337
Garden open to public. Retail.

Herbs-Liscious
1702 S. 6 Street
Marshalltown, Iowa 50158
(515) 752-4976
Garden open to public. Wholesale; retail. Mail/phone order. Catalog $2 (refundable with first order).

Hillside Herb Farm
RR 1, Box 151
Millbach Village
Newmanstown, Pennsylvania 17073
(717) 949-3086
Garden open to public. Retail. Catalog $3.

Hilltop Herbery
4748 Syracuse Road
Cazenovia, New York 13035
(315) 655-8812

Garden open to public (by appointment). Retail.

JoHanna's Cellar Babies
2575 Dogwood Drive
Youngstown, Ohio 44511-1311
(216) 793-9523
Wholesale; retail. Mail/phone order. Catalog $2 (refundable with first order).

Kathleen Gips' Village Herb Shop/Pine Creek Herbs
49 W. Orange Street
Chagrin Falls, Ohio 44022
(216) 247-0733
Retail. Mail/phone order. Catalog/handbook $4.

Ladybug Press
7348 Lane Park Court
Dallas, Texas 75225
(214) 368-4235
Retail. Mail/phone order.

Lambs & Thyme at Randallane
240 Bullock Road
Richmond, New Hampshire 03470
(603) 239-8621
Garden open to public. Wholesale; retail. Mail/phone order. Catalog, SASE; newsletter.

The Lavender Garden
120 McCracken Road
Danville, Pennsylvania 17821
(717) 275-8838
Garden open to public. Wholesale plants and soaps; retail.

Little Herb 'n Annie
PO Box 76, Route 53
Drifting, Pennsylvania 16834
(814) 345-6749
Garden open to public. Retail. Customer newsletter.

Louise Downey — Herbalist
Route 12
Bethel, Vermont 05032

Making Thyme Herb Shoppe, Ltd.
215 W. Main Street
Greenwood, Indiana 46142
(317) 889-4395
Wholesale; retail. Mail/phone order. Catalog $3; quarterly newsletter ($1.25 each).

Mari-Mann Herb Co., Inc.
N. end of St. Louis Bridge Road
Decatur, Illinois 62521-9404
(217) 429-1404
Garden open to public. Wholesale; retail. Mail/phone order. Catalog $2; newsletter.

Mountain Rose Herbs
PO Box 2000, Briceland Road
Redway, California 95560
(800) 879-3337
Garden open to public (by appointment). Wholesale; retail. Mail/phone order. Catalog $1.

Piccadilly Herb Club
614 Dorseyville Road
Pittsburgh, Pennsylvania 15238
(412) 487-2343

Garden open to public. Mail/phone order. Cookbook available for $14.00 (plus $2.25 postage and handling).

Prairie Trail Farm
16206 CR 40
Goshen, Indiana 46526
(219) 642-3555
Garden open to public. Wholesale; retail. Mail/phone order.

Rainbow's End Herbs
10084 Hooker Hill Road
Perrysburg, New York 14129
(716) 532-6022
Garden open to public. Wholesale; retail. Mail/phone order. Catalog $1.

Rasland Farm
NC 82 at US 13
Godwin, North Carolina 28344-9712
(910) 567-2705
Garden open to public. Retail. Mail/phone order. Catalog $3.

Richland Creek Herb Farm
4749 Joel Jessop Road
Seagrove, North Carolina 27341
(910) 879-2545
Garden open to public. Wholesale; retail. Free catalog.

Rose Manor Bed and Breakfast
124 South Linden Street
Manheim, Pennsylvania 17545
(717)664-4932;
(800)666-4932

Wholesale catalog with SASE; retail shop.

The Rosemary House, Inc.
120 S. Market Street
Mechanicsburg, Pennsylvania 17055
(717) 697-5111
Garden open to public. Wholesale; retail. Mail/phone order. Catalog $3.

Secret Garden Herb Shoppe
34 Barnstead Dr., Box 9
Springville, New York 14141-1069
(716) 592-9883
Retail. Mail order. Catalog $1.

Simpson's Country Herb Farm
11832 Jefferson Highway, SE
Jefferson, Oregon 97352
(503) 378-1545
Garden open to public. Retail. Mail/phone order. Catalog $1.

Stillwater Herb Farm
RD 5, Box 222E
Lewes, Delaware 19958
(302) 645-8789
Garden open to public. Retail. Quarterly newsletter.

Sunrise Herb Farm
85 Dodgingtown Road
Bethel, Connecticut 06801
(203) 794-0809
Garden open to public. Retail.

Sweet Posie Herbary
  300 Mill Street
  Johnsonburg, Pennsylvania
    15845-1506
  (814) 965-2873
Garden open to public. Retail.
Mail/phone order. Free catalog;
newsletter.

Sweet Remembrances
  118 S. Market Street
  Mechanicsburg, Pennsylvania
    17055
  (717) 697-5785
Garden open to public (tours
arranged).

Tea & Herb Essence
  476 Thames Street
  Newport, Rhode Island 02840
  (401) 847-7423
Garden open to public. Whole-
sale; retail. Mail/phone order.
Free catalog.

Thomson Herb Farm Food
    Emporium
  RR 1, Box 118
  Holliday, Missouri 65258
  (816) 266-3275;
  Fax: (816) 266-3436
Garden open to public. Retail.

Thorp's Igloo Grown Herbs
  Box 185A, RR 1
  Atlantic, Pennsylvania 16111
  (814) 425-7382

Garden open to public. Retail.
Mail/phone order (dried herbs,
herbal products). Catalog 75¢.

Thyme & Seasons Books
  PO Drawer M
  Bertram, Texas 78605
  (512) 355-2799
Wholesale; retail. Mail order.

Thyme Remembered
  8550 E. 32nd Place
  Tulsa, Oklahoma 74145
  (918) 627-8464
Garden open to public (by
appointment). Retail. Mail/
phone order. Catalog $1.

Underwood Herbs
  RR 2, Box 540
  Chateaugay, New York
  (518) 425-3306
Wholesale; retail. Mail/phone
order. Catalog, SASE.

United Society of Shakers
  RR 1, Box 640
  Poland Spring, Maine 04274
  (207) 926-4597
Wholesale; retail. Free catalog.

Victorian Herb Gardens
  8378 Dewey Road
  Cattaraugus, New York 14719
  (716) 257-9259;
  Fax: (716) 257-9490
Garden open to public. Retail.
Mail order. Catalog $1.

Village Herb Shop
  1151 Division Highway, Box 173
  Blue Ball, Pennsylvania
    17506
  (717) 354-6494
Garden open to public. Retail.
Mail/phone order. Catalog $1.

Walk In Beauty
  PO Box 1331
  Colfax, California 95713
  (916) 346-7143
Retail. Mail/phone order.
Catalog $1.

Weaver Creek Herbs
  PO Box 2310, 306 Main Street
  Weaverville, California 96093
  (916) 623-5734
Retail.

Woodland Herb Gardens
  5376 NE 132nd Avenue
  Spicer, Minnesota 56288
  (612) 796-5931
Guided group tours by appoint-
ment. Quarterly newsletter.

Woodland Herbs
  7741 N. Manitou Trail
  Northport, Michigan
  (616) 386-5081
Garden open to public. Retail.

State-by-State Listing of Recipe Contributors

ALABAMA

Arie's Herb Gardens

ARIZONA

Herbal Essence

ARKANSAS

Clement Herb Farm

CALIFORNIA

Dry Creek Herb Farm and
  Learning Center
Mountain Rose Herbs
Walk In Beauty
Weaver Creek Herbs

CONNECTICUT

Good Thyme Farm
Sunrise Herb Farm

DELAWARE

Stillwater Herb Farm

FLORIDA

Herb Society of Palm Beach
  County

ILLINOIS

Mari-Mann Herb Co., Inc.

INDIANA

Making Thyme Herb Shoppe,
  Ltd.
Prairie Trail Farm

IOWA

Herbs-Liscious

KENTUCKY

The Herb Market

MAINE

Broadacres Herbs
United Society of Shakers

MASSACHUSETTS

Bittersweet Herb Farm
Cricket Hill Herb Farm
Earthshine Herb & Book Shop

MICHIGAN

Woodland Herbs

MINNESOTA

Woodland Herb Gardens

MISSOURI

Thomson Herb Farm Food
  Emporium

NEW HAMPSHIRE

Lambs & Thyme at Randallane

NEW YORK

Frog Park Herbs
Hilltop Herbery
Rainbow's End Herbs
Secret Garden Herb Shoppe
Underwood Herbs
Victorian Herb Gardens

NORTH CAROLINA

Goldenrod Mountain Herbs
Rasland Farm
Richland Creek Herb Farm

OHIO

Becker's Cottage Garden Herb
  Farm
Herbal Lakes
JoHanna's Cellar Babies
Kathleen Gips' Village Herb
  Shop/Pine Creek Herbs

OKLAHOMA

Thyme Remembered

OREGON

Elderflower Farm
Simpson's Country Herb Farm

PENNSYLVANIA

Hillside Herb Farm
The Lavender Garden
Little Herb 'n Annie
Piccadilly Herb Club
Rose Manor Bed & Breakfast
The Rosemary House, Inc.

Sweet Posie Herbary
Sweet Remembrances
Thorp's Igloo Grown Herbs
Village Herb Shop

RHODE ISLAND

Herbs etc
Tea & Herb Essence

TEXAS

Devonshire Apothecary
Ladybug Press
Thyme & Seasons Books

VERMONT

Louise Downey — Herbalist

VIRGINIA

Captain Morgan's Herbs

Converting Recipe Measurements to Metric

Use the following formulas for converting U.S. measurements to
metric. Since the conversions are not exact, it's important to
convert the measurements for all of the ingredients to maintain
the same proportions as the original recipe.

When The Measurement Given Is	Multiply It By	To Convert To
teaspoons	4.93	milliliters
tablespoons	14.79	milliliters
fluid ounces	29.57	milliliters
cups	236.59	milliliters
cups	.236	liters
pints	473.18	milliliters
pints	.473	liters
quarts	946.36	milliliters
quarts	.946	liters
gallons	3.785	liters
ounces	28.35	grams
pounds	.454	kilograms
inches	2.54	centimeters
degrees Fahrenheit	$\frac{5}{9}$ (temperature – 32)	degrees Celsius (Centigrade)

RELATED BOOKS FROM STOREY PUBLISHING/GARDEN WAY PUBLISHING

Growing and Using Herbs Successfully by Betty E.M. Jacobs. Guide to planting, propagating, harvesting, drying, freezing, and storing 64 popular herbs. 240 pages.

At Home with Herbs: Inspiring Ideas for Cooking, Crafts, Decorating and Cosmetics by Jane Newdick. Over 1000 herbal projects for crafters, home decoraters, chefs, and naturalists. Includes information on planting, harvesting, and storing herbs. 224 pages.

The Herb Gardener: A Guide for All Seasons, by Susan McClure. Comprehensive, full-color handbook on planting and caring for more than 75 herbs. Includes herb garden designs. 240 pages.

The Herbal Tea Garden: Planning, Planting, Harvesting & Brewing by Marietta Marshall Marcin. Complete handbook for herbal tea lovers who want to select, grow, and create their own special brews from 70 herbal tea plants. 224 pages.

Herbal Treasures: Inspiring Month-by-Month Projects for Gardening, Cooking, and Crafts by Phyllis V. Shaudys. A compendium of the best herb crafts, recipes, and gardening ideas from herb experts across the country. 320 pages.

Herbal Vinegar by Maggie Oster. Instructions for making inexpensive and easy herb, spice, vegetable, and flower vinegars, along with more than 100 recipes for using them in everything from appetizers, soups, and salsas, to entrees. 172 pages.

Making & Using Dried Foods by Phyllis Hobson. Step-by-step instructions for drying fruits, vegetables, herbs, meats, and dairy products with or without a commercial dehydrator. Over 200 recipes using dried foods. 192 pages.

The Pleasure of Herbs: A Month-by-Month Guide to Growing, Using, and Enjoying Herbs by Phyllis Shaudys. Packed full of information about herbs and herb growing, with indoor and outdoor herb-growing directions, recipes, and craft projects for every month of the year. 288 pages.

These books are available at your bookstore, lawn and garden center, or directly from Storey Publishing, Department WM, Schoolhouse Road, Pownal, Vermont 05261. To order toll-free by phone, call 800-441-5700.

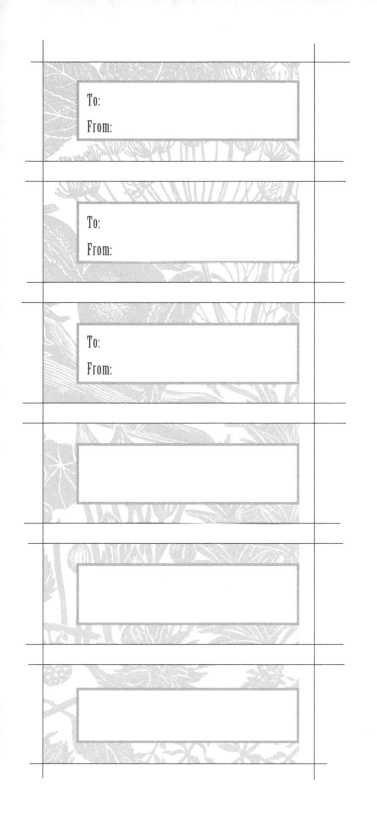

To:

From:

To:

From:

To:

From:

Blend Name:

Suggested Uses:

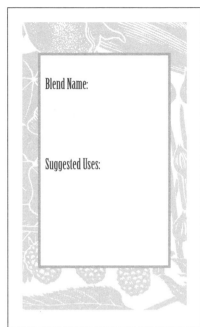

Blend Name:

Suggested Uses:

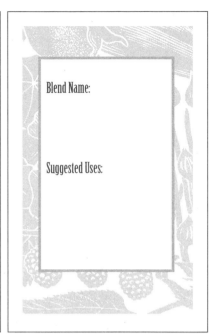

Blend Name:

Suggested Uses:

Blend Name:

Suggested Uses:

INDEX